Best of the

3 INGREDIENT

COOKBOOKS

by

Ruthie Wornall

2172-96

The Best of the 3 Ingredient Cookbooks

This book contains 365 fast, easy, tasty, and economical 3 ingredient recipes which I consider to be the "Best" from the series of nine cookbooks which I have written.

I began collecting these simple recipes soon after Jim and I were married when I discovered that he not only expected a hot dinner each evening but also expected me to entertain! Remembering the expression, "Necessity is the mother of invention," I began collecting 3 ingredient recipes that were so easy I couldn't ruin them.

This is a cookbook for the Nineties! A boon for busy people who do not have hours to spend in the kitchen, but who want to prepare nutritious meals in a hurry! This book is great for new brides, career people, college students, retired people, for children who are learning to cook and for those with disabilities. Even gourmet cooks occasionally need fast and easy recipes!

What pleases me most about my series of Three Ingredient Cookbooks is that they have been helpful to people. They have been transcribed into braille, used in school home economic classes, in hospice programs, mental health departments, in nursing home cooking classes, by those suffering from chronic fatigue syndrome, as well as by many busy people from all walks of life.

This book contains kitchen tested recipes in all categories ranging from appetizers and beverages for parties to soups, salads, vegetables, main dishes, breads, and desserts which enable you to prepare entire dinners in a hurry. The book incorporates shortcuts into many of the recipes which saves time, but does not compromise taste.

As mentioned earlier the book contains 365 recipes. You could prepare a new recipe each day of the year!

When you use these 3 ingredient recipes you won't mind inviting your Sunday School Class or your in-laws to your home for dinner—because now it is EASY TO COOK!

Listed below is a menu which can be prepared in 10 minutes (not counting cooking time) and it's good enough for company!

Judy's Orange Onion Chicken
Pecan Rice Pilaf
Rogene's Cherry-Cranberry Salad
Audrey's Green Beans
Ann's Chocolate-Cherry Cake

Happy Cooking!
Ruthie Wornall

Ruthie Wornall has been collecting easy recipes for nearly twenty years. She admits she was not a good cook when she was first married, but says these easy recipes helped it appear that she was. Her recipes are so fast and easy that she often prepares an entire dinner on television in ten minutes.

Ruthie, a former school teacher in Raytown, Missouri, is married to Jim Wornall, a second vice president at a corporation in Overland Park, Kansas, and they have two children who are still in school.

Ruthie writes the "Reluctant Chef" food column for the Weston Chronicle Newspaper in Weston, Missouri, as well as the "Recipe Corner" food column for the Newton County Times Newspaper in Jasper, Arkansas. She is active in a Baptist church, and volunteers weekly at a nursing home where her children occasionally sing and play piano for the residents.

Ruthie has written a series of ten cookbooks. They are: the Three Ingredient Cookbook, Volumes I, II, and III; the Low Cholesterol Three Ingredient Cookbook; the Three Ingredient Party Cookbook; the Three Ingredient Main Dish Cookbook; the Two Ingredient Cookbook; The Low-Fat Three Ingredient Cookbook, and the Low Sugar 3 Ingredient Cookbook.

The most recent book, The Best of the 3 Ingredient Cookbook is now available.

THIS BOOK includes the finest plastic ring binders available, BUT, like most plastics, the BINDERS CAN BE DAMAGED BY EXCESSIVE HEAT, so AVOID exposing them to the direct rays of the SUN, or excessive heat such as IN A CAR on a hot day, or on the top of the kitchen STOVE. If not exposed to heat, the binders will last indefinitely.

R. K. Smith—Photographer
Weekly Vista
Bella Vista, Arkansas

A Word of Thanks ...

*"A recipe not shared with others
will soon be forgotten."*

I wish to express my sincere appreciation and thanks to all those individuals who donated recipes or in any other way contributed to the publication of this cookbook.

Special thanks to the following people who helped me kitchen test and taste these recipes: Lois Davis, Tessa McKee, Jim Wornall, John Wornall, and Velora Holt.

TABLE OF CONTENTS

FAVORITE RECIPES
FROM MY COOKBOOK

Recipe Name	Page Number

Appetizers,
Beverages

FOOD QUANTITIES FOR 25, 50, AND 100 SERVINGS

FOOD	25 SERVINGS	50 SERVINGS	100 SERVINGS
Rolls	4 doz.	8 doz.	16 doz.
Bread	50 slices or 3 1-lb. loaves	100 slices or 6 1-lb. loaves	200 slices or 12 1-lb. loaves
Butter	½ lb.	¾ to 1 lb.	1½ lb.
Mayonnaise	1 c.	2 to 3 c.	4 to 6 c.
Mixed filling for sandwiches (meat, eggs, fish)	1½ qt.	2½ to 3 qt.	5 to 6 qt.
Mixed filling (sweet-fruit)	1 qt.	1¾ to 2 qt.	2½ to 4 qt.
Jams & preserves	1½ lb.	3 lb.	6 lb
Crackers	1½ lb.	3 lb.	6 lb.
Cheese (2 oz. per serving)	3 lb.	6 lb.	12 lb.
Soup	1½ gal.	3 gal.	6 gal.
Salad dressings	1 pt.	2½ pt.	½ gal.
Meat, Poultry, or Fish:			
Wieners (beef)	6½ lb.	13 lb.	25 lb.
Hamburger	9 lb.	18 lb.	35 lb.
Turkey or chicken	13 lb.	25 to 35 lb.	50 to 75 lb.
Fish, large whole (round)	13 lb.	25 lb.	50 lb.
Fish, fillets or steaks	7½ lb.	15 lb.	30 lb.
Salads, Casseroles, Vegetables:			
Potato salad	4¼ qt.	2¼ gal.	4½ gal.
Scalloped potatoes	4½ qt. or 1 12x20" pan	8½ qt.	17 qt.
Mashed potatoes	9 lb.	18-20 lb.	25-35 lb.
Spaghetti	1¼ gal.	2½ gal.	5 gal.
Baked beans	¾ gal.	1¼ gal.	2½ gal.
Jello salad	¾ gal.	1¼ gal.	2½ gal.
Canned vegetables	1 #10 can	2½ #10 cans	4 #10 cans
Fresh Vegetables:			
Lettuce (for salads)	4 heads	8 heads	15 heads
Carrots (3 oz. or ½ c.)	6¼ lb.	12½ lb.	25 lb.
Tomatoes	3-5 lb.	7-10 lb.	14-20 lb.
Desserts:			
Watermelon	37½ lb.	75 lb.	150 lb.
Fruit cup (½ c. per serving)	3 qt.	6 qt.	12 qt.
Cake	1 10x12" sheet cake	1 12x20" sheet cake	2 12x20" sheet cakes
	1½ 10" layer cakes	3 10" layer cakes	6 10" layer cakes
Whipping cream	¾ pt.	1½ to 2 pt.	3 pt.
Ice Cream:			
Brick	3¼ qt.	6½ qt.	12½ qt.
Bulk	2¼ qt.	4½ qt. or 1¼ gal.	9 qt. or 2½ gal.
Beverages:			
Coffee	½ lb. and 1½ gal. water	1 lb. and 3 gal. water	2 lb. and 6 gal. water
Tea	1/12 lb. and 1½ gal. water	⅙ lb. and 3 gal. water	⅓ lb. and 6 gal. water
Lemonade	10 to 15 lemons, 1½ gal. water	20 to 30 lemons, 3 gal. water	40 to 60 lemons, 6 gal. water

APPETIZERS, BEVERAGES

CUCUMBER TEA SANDWICHES

2 cucumbers, peeled,
   seeded, and grated
2 (3 oz.) pkg. cream cheese,
   softened

Bread, sliced thin and crusts
   removed

Combine and mix cream cheese and 1½ grated cucumbers until well blended. Spread on bread. Cut bread in triangle or diamond shapes or in bars.

Garnish each sandwich with a thin cucumber slice from the remaining ½ cucumber.

SAUSAGE BALLS

2 c. Bisquick mix
1 lb. hot sausage (R.B. Rice)

1 c. shredded Cheddar
   cheese

Mix the 3 ingredients together with wooden spoon or your hands. Shape into balls. Place on jelly roll pan and bake at 350°F. for 20 minutes. These freeze well. Makes about 3 dozen small balls.

TUNA BALL

1 (8 oz.) pkg. cream cheese, softened
½ pkg. Lipton dry onion soup mix

1 (6¼ oz.) can white albacore tuna, drained (or any tuna you prefer)

Combine ingredients; mix well. Shape into a ball. Chill 4 to 6 hours.

Serve with crackers, chips, or raw vegetables. Serves 8.

EASY CHEESE BALL

2 small jars Old English sharp cheese
Nuts, finely chopped

2 (3 oz.) pkg. cream cheese, softened

Combine cheese and cream cheese. Mix well, then shape into a ball. Chill 4 to 6 hours.

Roll cheese ball in chopped nuts. Wrap in Saran Wrap until time to serve. Serves 8.

ARTICHOKE DIP

1 can drained artichoke
  hearts, chopped

1 c. Parmesan cheese
1 c. mayonnaise

Combine the 3 ingredients; mix well and pour into a greased baking dish. Bake 20 to 30 minutes at 350°F.

Serve with fresh vegetables, chips or crackers. Serves 8 to 12.

SHRIMP SURPRISE

¼ c. shrimp cocktail sauce
  (or more)
1 (8 oz.) pkg. Philadelphia
  cream cheese

1 to 2 cans tiny shrimp,
  cooked, drained, and
  chilled

Place bar of cream cheese in center of a serving plate. Pour cocktail sauce over cheese. Sprinkle cooled shrimp over sauce. Surround with crackers. Serves 8 to 12.

BLACK OLIVE SPREAD

1 small can chopped black
 olives
1 (8 oz.) pkg. shredded
 Cheddar cheese

1 (3 oz.) pkg. Philadelphia
 cream cheese

Combine olives and the 2 cheeses. (Optional: Mix in 3 chopped green onions.)

Spread on slices of party rye or pumpernickel bread. Serve cold, or broil and serve hot. Serves 6 to 8.

CHILI CON QUESO

1 lb. Velveeta cheese
1 (10 oz.) can Ro-Tel
 tomatoes, drained

1 to 2 chopped green onions
 or chives

Melt Velveeta cheese in top of double boiler. Stir in 1 can drained Ro-Tel tomatoes. Sprinkle chopped green onions or chives over top.

Serve with Fritos or tortilla chips. Serves 8 to 12.

MARY SUTTON'S SALAMI-OLIVE WRAPS

8 salami slices
1 to 2 (3 oz.) pkg. cream
   cheese, softened

1 small jar green olives
   (stuffed with pimento)

Cut salami into 2 to 3 inch strips. Spread each strip with softened Philadelphia cream cheese. Place one olive in center of salami strip. Roll up and hold with wooden pick. Makes about 24.

ANN'S BACON WRAPPED CHESTNUTS

1 (8 oz.) can whole water
   chestnuts, drained

½ lb. bacon, cut in halves
¼ c. soy sauce

Marinate water chestnuts for an hour or more in soy sauce. Wrap ½ bacon slice around chestnut and fasten with a wooden pick. Bake at 375°F. for 20 to 25 minutes. Makes about 30.

LUCY HETZEL'S FRESH FRUIT DIP

1 (8 oz.) pkg. cream cheese, softened

1 (7 oz.) jar marshmallow creme
¼ tsp. ginger

Combine and mix well. Serve as a dip surrounded by fresh fruits (strawberries, banana slices, etc.). Makes 2 cups.

SAUSAGE-CHEESE SNACKS

1 loaf party rye bread
1 lb. hot spicy sausage

1 lb. Cheddar cheese, cut in 1 inch squares

Freeze bread. Spread bread with raw sausage. Top with 1 inch square thin slice of cheese. Lay on greased cookie sheet with edges or on a jelly roll pan. Bake for 20 minutes at 350°. Makes about 25 snacks.

HAMBURGER-CHEESE DIP

2 lb. Velveeta cheese
1 lb. hamburger, browned
    and drained

1 (10 oz.) can Ro-Tel
    tomatoes, drained

     Melt cheese. Stir in meat and tomatoes. Serve hot with large Fritos corn chips.

PIGS IN BLANKETS

1 pkg. of 10 hot dogs
3 cans biscuits (10 biscuit
    size)

Mustard (Dijon)

     Cut hot dogs in thirds. Wrap in biscuit that has been spread with mustard. Bake at 425°F. for 8 to 10 minutes. Makes 30.

SAUCY BARBECUED SAUSAGES

1 pkg. Hillshire Farm fully
   cooked sausage (50
   per pkg.)

1 (18 oz.) bottle barbecue
   sauce
1 (12 oz.) jar grape jelly

   Pour the barbecue sauce and the grape jelly into a large saucepan. Cook and stir until the jelly has melted and the mixture is smooth. Add the cooked smoked sausages and heat on low or simmer for an hour, stirring often. Serve hot. This could be served in a crock pot. Makes 50.

   Optional: Wieners could be substituted for the sausages. They should be cut in 1 inch pieces and cooked.

SPEEDY JALAPENO APPETIZERS

1 box Ritz or Hi-Ho crackers
1 (8 oz.) pkg. cream cheese,
   softened

1 small jar green jalapeno
   jelly

   Spread softened cream cheese on crackers. Spoon a small amount of jalapeno jelly in the middle of each cracker. Serve immediately.

CAVIAR SPREAD

**1 (8 oz.) pkg. cream cheese
(Philadelphia Brand)**

**1 red onion, chopped
1 jar black caviar**

Place the cream cheese in the center of a plate. Sprinkle chopped red onion over cheese, then heap caviar on top. Serves 6 to 8.

Serve with Melba toast rounds.

SHRIMP APPETIZER TREE

**Shrimp, deveined and
cooked
Parsley or endive**

Lemon wedges

Completely cover a styrofoam cone with parsley or endive anchored securely with floral wire picks. Secure cone to plate with floral sticky tape. Cover plate with parsley or endive. Insert colored party picks through shrimp and onto the styrofoam cone. Serve with lemon wedges surrounding the shrimp "tree."

SAUNDRA GARRETT'S CRAB SPREAD

1 (8 oz.) pkg. fat free cream
    cheese, softened
1 (4 oz.) can crabmeat,
    drained and flaked

½ (8 oz.) bottle cocktail
    sauce

Shape softened cream cheese into a cross for Easter, a heart for Valentine's Day, a Christmas tree for Christmas, or whatever you wish. Place cheese in center of a platter. Pour cocktail sauce over cream cheese, then sprinkle crabmeat over sauce. Serve with reduced calorie Ritz crackers. Serves 8.

JOHN WORNALL'S TORTILLA CHIPS AND DIP

1 pkg. corn tortillas
¼ tsp. cumin seasoning

1 (16 oz.) jar thick and
    chunky salsa

Cut a stack of 10 tortillas into 8 wedges each. Spread these "pie-shaped" wedges on a baking sheet that has been sprayed with a nonstick cooking spray. Sprinkle lightly with cumin. Bake at 375°F. for 5 minutes. Turn and bake 5 minutes longer or until chips are crisp. Watch carefully that they do not burn. Cool. Yield: 80 chips or about 4 servings. Serve with salsa.

RED CABBAGE BASKET OF DIP

Red cabbage　　　　　　　　**12 oz. sour cream**
Lipton dry onion soup mix

Combine dry onion soup mix with sour cream. Mix the dip well.

Cut top off of a washed red cabbage. Hollow out to form a basket or cup. Fill with onion dip.

Place in center of platter and surround it with fresh veggies: Carrot sticks, celery, olives, zucchini sticks, etc. Or serve with chips or Fritos if preferred. Serves 12.

CHIPPED BEEF BALLS

1 (4 oz.) pkg. chipped beef　　　**1 to 2 Tbsp. chopped onion**
2 (3 oz.) pkg. cream cheese

Spread a thin layer of chipped beef in a shallow pan; place in a 350°F. oven until dry and crisp, about 15 minutes. Cool. Crumble dried beef. Set aside.

Combine cream cheese and onion. Shape into small balls. Roll in crumbled dried beef until beef coats the balls. Serve on wooden picks. Makes 1½ to 2 dozen.

CROCK POT MEXICAN DIP

2 lb. Velveeta cheese
1 lb. (R.B. Rice) sausage

1 (10 oz.) can undrained Ro-
    Tel tomatoes

Brown, crumble, and drain sausage.

Place Velveeta cheese in the crock pot and heat until cheese melts, then stir in well-drained sausage. Add Ro-Tel tomatoes, heat through, and mix well.

Serve hot with tortilla chips or large Fritos.

CREAM CHEESE AND BEEF BALL

1 (8 oz.) pkg. cream cheese,
    softened
1 bunch green onions,
    chopped

2 pkg. chipped beef,
    chopped fine

Combine and mix well. Shape into a ball. Refrigerate.

CHEESE STRAWS

1 (5 oz.) pkg. pie crust mix
½ c. shredded Cheddar cheese

Red pepper to taste

Prepare pie crust dough according to package directions. Roll out dough on a floured board into a rectangular shape. Sprinkle cheese over it, then sprinkle red pepper over cheese. Fold dough over once to cover cheese, then roll out again to a rectangle ¼ inch thick. Cut dough into 3 x ½ inch strips and place them on a lightly greased cookie sheet. Bake for 10 to 15 minutes at 350°F.

STUFFED MUSHROOMS

1 lb. sausage
1 lb. large mushrooms

½ pkg. Lipton onion soup mix

Remove stems and wash caps. Combine sausage and dry onion soup mix. Stuff each cap with a mound of sausage mixture. Place on a baking sheet with sides. Bake for 20 minutes at 350°F. Drain well.

BROCCOLI-MUSHROOM DIP

1 (10¾ oz.) can golden
   mushroom soup
1 tube Kraft garlic cheese

1 (10 oz.) frozen box
   chopped broccoli

Melt cheese. Stir in soup, then chopped broccoli. Heat thoroughly. Serve with raw vegetables or Fritos.

HOT APPLE CIDER

2 qt. apple cider
1 apple, sliced

½ c. cinnamon red hot
   candies

Pour 2 quarts apple cider into a large pan. Stir in ½ cup red hot candies. Simmer until candy has dissolved.

Serve hot in mugs. Garnish with ½ apple slice. Makes 2 quarts.

CRANBERRY PUNCH

2 qt. chilled cranberry juice
2 qt. chilled ginger ale or 7-
   Up

2 small cans frozen
   lemonade concentrate

    Combine, mix, and pour into punch bowl. Add 2 to 4 cans water, if needed. Makes about 1 gallon.

BETTY'S HAWAIIAN PUNCH

1 (46 oz.) can Hawaiian
   punch, chilled
1 (2 liter) bottle chilled
   ginger ale or 7-Up

1 (12 oz.) can frozen
   lemonade concentrate

    Combine the ingredients in a punch bowl. Mix in 4 cups cold water. Makes 20 to 24 cups of punch.

STRAWBERRY PUNCH

2 (6 oz.) cans frozen pink
    lemonade concentrate
2 (10 oz.) boxes
    strawberries, frozen

1 (2 liter) bottle 7-Up or
    ginger ale, chilled

Thaw berries until slushy (or mix in blender). Pour lemonade into punch bowl and stir in berries. Add 7-Up or ginger ale and stir until well blended. (If this punch is too tart, you might wish to add sugar.) Serves 20 to 25.

ANNA MARIE'S LOW-CAL PUNCH

1 (2 liter) diet 7-Up, chilled
1 (12 oz.) can frozen *Minute
    Maid* lemonade

1 (46 oz.) can unsweetened
    Dole pineapple juice,
    chilled

Combine in punch bowl and mix well. (Recipe can be doubled.) Add an ice ring to the punch bowl, if you wish. Makes about 25 (4 ounce) cups.

BARBARA'S PINEAPPLE PUNCH

4 qt. ginger ale, chilled
2 qt. pineapple sherbet

1 (15 oz.) can pineapple
    tidbits, chilled

Combine ginger ale, pineapple sherbet, and pineapple tidbits. Mix. Serve in punch bowl. Serves about 30.

LIME SHERBET PUNCH

½ gal. lime sherbet
1 (2 liter) bottle 7-Up, chilled

1 (2 liter) bottle ginger ale,
    chilled

Combine, mix, and serve in punch bowl. Makes about 40 (4 ounce) cups.

SUN TEA

8 regular-size tea bags **Lemon slices or mint**
1 gal. cold water

Put 8 regular-size tea bags in a gallon jar and fill with cold water. Set jar in sunshine for 3 to 4 hours.

Serve over ice with lemon slice (*or* sprig of mint). Serves 8 to 12.

ROSEBILLIE'S COCOA MIX

3 c. dry powdered milk **⅓ c. cocoa**
1 c. sugar

Mix well.

Use 6 level tablespoons to each cup of hot water to make a cup of hot chocolate.

Optional: Top each cup with a marshmallow.

DOROTHY TOWNSEND'S
STRAWBERRY PUNCH

½ gal. strawberry ice cream,
    softened
2 (2 liter) bottles ginger ale
    or 7-Up, chilled

1 (10 oz.) pkg. frozen
    strawberries, thawed

Combine all ingredients in a punch bowl and stir well. Serve immediately.

CRANBERRY-GRAPE FROST

1 (48 oz.) bottle cranberry
    juice, chilled
1 (46 oz.) can grape juice,
    chilled

½ gal. vanilla ice cream or
    raspberry sherbet

Combine cranberry and grape juices in a punch bowl. Add scoops of vanilla ice cream and mix well. Serves about 20.

Optional: Add 1 (2 liter) bottle chilled ginger ale or 7-Up.

MOCHA PUNCH

1 qt. instant coffee, chilled
1 qt. chocolate milk

1 qt. vanilla or chocolate ice
   cream

Mix the coffee and milk together until well blended. Just before serving, stir in the ice cream and mix until creamy. Makes ½ gallon.

MARY'S D.A.R. PUNCH

2 qt. orange juice, chilled
2 qt. lemonade, chilled

1 or 2 (1 liter) bottles 7-Up,
   chilled

Combine and mix in a punch bowl.

Note: This punch was served at a D.A.R. meeting in Raytown, Missouri, during the spring of 1991. Makes about 20 cups of punch.

ONITA COPELAND'S GRAPE PUNCH

Grapes in a frozen ice ring of
    ginger ale (red
    seedless grapes)

1 gal. white grape juice
½ gal. ginger ale

    When ready to serve, mix juice and ginger ale in punch bowl. Add ice ring. Makes about 24 punch size cups.

REFRIGERATOR ICED TEA

8 tea bags (regular size)
2 qt. cold water

Lemon slices

    Rather than boiling water on hot, humid days, just add 8 tea bags to 2 quarts cold water. Place in refrigerator for 3 to 4 hours. Remove tea bags when ready to serve. Serve over ice with lemon slices. Serves 8.

CAROLYN WARREN'S
STRAWBERRY MILKSHAKE

½ c. fresh strawberries,
    sliced
½ c. skim milk

3 packets Equal sweetener

Combine berries, milk, and Equal in a blender and blend until smooth. Yield: 1 cup.

Optional: To make a thicker shake, you could add 3 ice cubes to the blender.

Also, if desired, you can substitute frozen unsweetened berries for the fresh ones.

Contains 63 calories and just a trace of fat grams.

CHRISTMAS PUNCH

1 (46 oz.) can pineapple juice,
    chilled
1 (1 liter) bottle ginger ale,
    chilled

1 (2 liter) bottle strawberry
    carbonated beverage,
    chilled

Combine and mix in punch bowl. (Use extra ginger ale or 7-Up, if desired.) Serves about 30.

WINTER PUNCH

1 (46 oz.) can V-8 juice, chilled
1 Tbsp. lemon juice

½ tsp. dried dill weed

Combine, mix, and serve chilled in glasses. Serves 6 to 8.

Optional: Put a long celery stick in each glass for stirring.

"If a recipe has more than 3 ingredients, it's not easy!"

Notes

Soups,
Salads

A HANDY SPICE AND HERB GUIDE

ALLSPICE-a pea-sized fruit that grows in Mexico, Jamaica, Central and South America. Its delicate flavor resembles a blend of cloves, cinnamon, and nutmeg. USES: (Whole) Pickles, meats, boiled fish, gravies; (Ground) Puddings, relishes, fruit preserves, baking.

BASIL-the dried leaves and stems of an herb grown in the United States and North Mediterranean area. Has an aromatic, leafy flavor. USES: For flavoring tomato dishes and tomato paste, turtle soup; also use in cooked peas, squash, snap beans; sprinkle chopped over lamb chops and poultry.

BAY LEAVES-the dried leaves of an evergreen grown in the eastern Mediterranean countries. Has a sweet, herbaceous floral spice note. USES: For pickling, stews, for spicing sauces and soup. Also use with a variety of meats and fish.

CARAWAY-the seed of a plant grown in the Netherlands. Flavor that combines the tastes of anise and dill. USES: For the cordial Kummel, baking breads; often added to sauerkraut, noodles, cheese spreads. Also adds zest to French fried potatoes, liver, canned asparagus.

CURRY POWDER-a ground blend of ginger, turmeric, fenugreek seed, as many as 16 to 20 spices. USES: For all Indian curry recipes such as lamb, chicken, and rice, eggs, vegetables, and curry puffs.

DILL-the small, dark seed of the dill plant grown in India, having a clean, aromatic taste. USES: Dill is a predominant seasoning in pickling recipes; also adds pleasing flavor to sauerkraut, potato salad, cooked macaroni, and green apple pie.

MACE-the dried covering around the nutmeg seed. Its flavor is similar to nutmeg, but with a fragrant, delicate difference. USES: (Whole) For pickling, fish, fish sauce, stewed fruit. (Ground) Delicious in baked goods, pastries, and doughnuts, adds unusual flavor to chocolate desserts.

MARJORAM-an herb of the mint family, grown in France and Chile. Has a minty-sweet flavor. USES: In beverages, jellies, and to flavor soups, stews, fish, sauces. Also excellent to sprinkle on lamb while roasting.

MSG (MONOSODIUM GLUTAMATE)-a vegetable protein derivative for raising the effectiveness of natural food flavors. USES: Small amounts, adjusted to individual taste, can be added to steaks, roasts, chops, seafoods, stews, soups, chowder, chop suey, and cooked vegetables.

OREGANO-a plant of the mint family and a species of marjoram of which the dried leaves are used to make an herb seasoning. USES: An excellent flavoring for any tomato dish, especially pizza, chili con carne, and Italian specialties.

PAPRIKA-a mild, sweet red pepper growing in Spain, Central Europe, and the United States. Slightly aromatic and prized for brilliant red color. USES: A colorful garnish for pale foods, and for seasoning Chicken Paprika, Hungarian Goulash, salad dressings.

POPPY-the seed of a flower grown in Holland. Has a rich fragrance and crunchy, nut-like flavor. USES: Excellent as a topping for breads, rolls, and cookies. Also delicious in buttered noodles.

ROSEMARY-an herb (like a curved pine needle) grown in France, Spain, and Portugal, and having a sweet fresh taste. USES: In lamb dishes, in soups, stews, and to sprinkle on beef before roasting.

SAGE-the leaf of a shrub grown in Greece, Yugoslavia, and Albania. Flavor is camphoraceous and minty. USES: For meat and poultry stuffing, sausages, meat loaf, hamburgers, stews, and salads.

THYME-the leaves and stems of a shrub grown in France and Spain. Has a strong, distinctive flavor. USES: For poultry seasoning, croquettes, fricassees, and fish dishes. Also tasty on fresh sliced tomatoes.

TURMERIC-a root of the ginger family, grown in India, Haiti, Jamaica, and Peru, having a mild, ginger-pepper flavor. USES: As a flavoring and coloring in prepared mustard and in combination with mustard as a flavoring for meats, dressings, salads.

SOUPS, SALADS

EASY STEAK SOUP

1 or 2 lb. ground round steak
1 (46 oz.) can V-8 juice

1 (20 oz.) pkg. frozen
   vegetables

    Brown ground round steak and drain. Combine V-8 juice and frozen vegetables with meat and bring to boil. Simmer 20 minutes. Serves 6 to 8.

    Optional: Add chopped onion.

NO-PEEK STEW

2 lb. beef stew meat, cubed
   and fat trimmed

1 (10 oz.) can mushroom
   soup
1 pkg. onion soup mix

    Combine and mix well. Stir in 1 cup water. Cover; bake for 2½ to 3 hours at 300° to 325°. *Do not peek!* Optional: Serve over rice or noodles. Serves 6.

TOMATO-BACON SOUP

1 (10 oz.) can Campbell's
    tomato soup
1 (16 oz.) can stewed
    tomatoes (with celery
    and peppers)

½ lb. bacon, fried, drained,
    and crumbled

Combine soup and stewed tomatoes. Heat thoroughly. Sprinkle bacon over soup and serve hot. Serves 4.

Good with grilled cheese sandwiches.

PINTO BEAN SOUP

2 (1 lb.) pkg. dry pinto beans
Salt to taste

Smoked ham hocks or
    chopped ham

Wash beans. Cover with cold water and soak overnight.

Next day: Drain and recover beans with water. Bring to a boil. Add ham. Reduce heat and simmer slowly 3 to 4 hours. Season with salt. Serves 6.

Great with corn bread.

GUACAMOLE SOUP

1 (18 oz.) can spicy V-8
    tomato cocktail juice
2 peeled and seeded
    avocados, chopped

⅓ c. chopped onion

    Heat V-8 juice and onion for 5 minutes or until very hot. Stir in ¾ of all the diced avocado and heat. Reserve ¼ of it for garnish. Sprinkle it on top of soup. Serve immediately. Serves 4.

MINUTE STEW

1 lb. extra lean hamburger,
    browned, crumbled,
    and drained
1 (16 oz.) can Brook's diced
    tomatoes and onions

1 (11 oz.) can Green Giant
    white corn (or any can
    whole kernel corn)

    Combine browned and drained hamburger, tomatoes, and corn in a skillet and mix well. Simmer for 20 to 30 minutes, stirring often. Serves 4.

PAT'S CHILLED STRAWBERRY SOUP

2 (10 oz.) pkg. strawberries
    in syrup
½ c. cranberries

1 (8 oz.) ctn. nonfat
    strawberry yogurt

Combine in blender container and blend until smooth. Refrigerate 1 to 2 hours before serving. Serve chilled. Serves 6 to 8. Great summer soup!

PENNY SPARKS' CHICKEN AND NOODLES

4 to 6 chicken breasts, cubed
    and boiled
1 or 2 pkgs. no-yolk egg
    noodles

4 (10¾ oz.) cans low-fat
    cream of mushroom
    soup

Boil chicken (in enough water to cover) until tender. Add egg noodles and cook until tender.

Stir in cream of mushroom soup and heat thoroughly.

STEVE KIRK'S CORN SOUP

2 (16 oz.) cans whole kernel
   corn
2 to 3 Tbsp. Pace chunky
   salsa (or to taste)

2 to 3 Tbsp. peach preserves
   (or to taste)

Combine and mix well. Bring to boil. Reduce heat and simmer 5 minutes. Serves 4. (Try it! You'll like it!)

CLAM CHOWDER

1 (10¾ oz.) can New England
   clam chowder
1 (10¾ oz.) can cream of
   celery soup

1 (10¾ oz.) can cream of
   potato soup

Combine in saucepan and mix well. Heat and stir. (If it needs to be diluted, add milk.) Serves 4.

CHERRY-CRANBERRY MOLD

1 (6 oz.) pkg. cherry Jell-O
1 (21 oz.) can cherry pie
   filling

1 (16 oz.) can whole
   cranberry sauce

Prepare Jell-O as box directs, but decrease cold water by 1 cup. Mix cranberries and cherries into Jell-O. Pour into a mold or a 9x13 inch Pyrex dish and refrigerate until firm. Serves 8 to 10.

ROMAINE-ARTICHOKE SALAD

1 head romaine lettuce, torn
   in bite-size pieces
1 (16 oz.) can artichoke
   hearts, drained and
   chopped

1 large tomato, cut into
   wedges

Toss all ingredients together. Good with French dressing. Serves 4.

PAM'S CREAMY CRANBERRY MOLD

2 (3 oz.) pkg. cherry Jell-O   1 (16 oz.) can jellied
1 c. sour cream   cranberry sauce

    Dissolve Jell-O in 2 cups boiling water. Stir in cranberry sauce. Mix until well blended. Add sour cream and beat in an electric mixer until creamy. Pour into a mold and chill until firm. Serves 6 to 8.

WILMA DAVIS' CINNAMON APPLE SALAD

⅔ c. cinnamon red hot   1 (3 oz.) pkg. cherry Jell-O
    candies
1½ c. Musselman's
    applesauce

    Heat cinnamon red hots in ⅔ cup boiling water until candy melts. Pour over dry Jell-O and stir until well dissolved.

    Chill until partially set. Stir in applesauce. Refrigerate until firm. Serves 4.

CHICKEN SALAD VERONIQUE

2 c. diced, cooked chicken breasts

**1 c. seedless grapes
Mayonnaise**

Combine chicken, grapes, and mayonnaise. Mix well and chill.

Optional: Stir in ⅔ teaspoon curry powder (or slivered almonds). Serves 4.

STUFFED TOMATO SALAD

**4 to 6 tomatoes
Cottage cheese**

1 chopped onion

Cut each tomato ¾ of way down into 6 wedges, then separate wedges slightly. Turn upside down and drain on napkins. (Or cut off top of tomato and scoop out pulp, then drain.)

Combine cottage cheese and onion. Mix and fill tomato cavity.

For variation: Stuff tomatoes with tuna salad instead of cottage cheese. Serves 4 to 6.

CRANBERRY ORANGE RELISH

**1 (15 oz.) can whole berry
cranberries, drained**

**⅔ c. orange marmalade
⅓ c. black walnuts**

Combine, mix, cover, and chill 2 to 3 hours before serving. Serves 4.

Variation: Add 1 cup drained maraschino cherries.

SPINACH-ORANGE SALAD

**2 c. spinach, washed and
torn into pieces
⅓ c. toasted slivered
almonds**

**1 can mandarin oranges
(drain juice, but
reserve)**

Toss together. Sprinkle with juice from mandarin oranges. Serves 4.

Optional: Sprinkle with poppy seeds.

Optional: Toss with vinegar and oil dressing.

TUNA ARTICHOKE SALAD

2 (6 oz.) cans albacore white   Mayonnaise
    tuna fish (or any tuna)
1 (16 oz.) can artichoke
    hearts, drained and
    chopped

Drain tuna and flake. Chop artichokes. Combine and mix with enough mayonnaise to moisten. Serves 4.

Optional: Stir in slivered almonds.

Optional: Substitute cubed chicken breast for tuna.

Variation: Serve on toast as a sandwich.

STRAWBERRY-BANANA WHIP

1 (3 oz.) pkg. strawberry Jell-   2 sliced bananas
    O gelatin
1 (8 oz.) Cool Whip whipped
    topping

Prepare Jell-O with 1 cup boiling water and stir until dissolved. Add ½ cup cold water. Mix well. Chill until partially set.

Whip Jell-O, then mix in Cool Whip and blend. Stir in bananas. Cover and chill until firm. Serves 4.

Optional: Add chopped apples.

ANITA McKEE'S RASPBERRY SALAD

1 small pkg. sugar free
    raspberry gelatin
1 (10 oz.) pkg. frozen
    unsweetened raspberries

1 (8 oz.) ctn. Cool Whip Lite
    whipped topping

Prepare gelatin as package directs to dissolve it and mix well. Do not add any cold water. Cover and refrigerate until partially jelled. Beat with an electric mixer until fluffy. Fold in whipped topping and beat until blended. Stir in raspberries. Cover and refrigerate until firm. Serves 6.

ROMAINE AND MELON SALAD

2 c. romaine lettuce, cut in
    bite-size pieces
1 c. honeydew melon, cubed

1 c. watermelon or
    cantaloupe, cubed (or
    both)

Toss lettuce and melon cubes together in a salad bowl. Serves 4.

Serve with Judy's Honey-Lime Dressing.

ORANGE-CRANBERRY SALAD

1 small box orange Jell-O
1⅓ c. boiling water
1 (12 oz.) ctn. Ocean Spray
   ground Cran-Orange
   relish

Dissolve the orange gelatin in a bowl with 1⅓ cups boiling water. Stir in the cranberry relish. Cover and refrigerate until firm. Serves 4.

Optional: Pour into a mold before refrigerating.

BLUEBERRY SALAD

2 (3 oz.) boxes grape Jell-O   1 (20 oz.) can crushed
1 (21 oz.) can blueberry pie   pineapple (undrained)
   filling

Dissolve Jell-O as package directs, using 2 cups boiling water, but do *not* add cold water or ice cubes.

Refrigerate until partially set, then stir in blueberries, pineapple, and juice. Pour into a 9x13 inch Pyrex dish and chill until firm. Serves 8.

Optional: Add sliced bananas to salad when other fruit is added.

GREEK SUMMER SALAD

4 c. fresh spinach, torn in bite-size pieces

1½ c. sliced strawberries
⅓ c. Feta cheese

Combine and toss salad ingredients. Cover and refrigerate until serving time. Serves 4.

DESIREE'S FRUIT SALAD

1 (16 oz.) can chunky fruit salad
2 sliced bananas

1 c. red seedless grapes

Combine, mix, cover, and refrigerate until ready to serve. Serves 4.

JUDITH'S WALNUT-CRANBERRY RELISH

1 (16 oz.) can whole berry
    cranberries
1 (8 oz.) can crushed
    pineapple, drained

½ c. chopped black walnuts

Combine, mix, and chill.

May double recipe.

BETTY MARCASON'S RED HOT APPLES

6 Jonathan apples
1 pkg. "red hots" cinnamon
    candies

Water

Peel and slice apples ¼ to ½ inch thick. Place in saucepan and pour red hots over them. Add enough water to cover apples. Bring to a boil. Reduce heat, then simmer until apples are tender. Apples will turn red and have a wonderful "red hot" cinnamon taste.

MARGARET SINCLAIR'S
CARROT-PINEAPPLE JELLO SALAD

1 (3 oz.) box orange or lime
   jello
½ c. grated carrots

1 (8 oz.) can crushed
   pineapple, drained

    Prepare jello according to package directions. Refrigerate until partially jelled. Stir in carrots and pineapple. Chill for several hours before serving.

JAN'S VANILLA FRUIT SALAD

2 cans chunky fruit (not fruit
   cocktail)
2 sliced bananas

1 (6 oz.) pkg. dry instant
   vanilla pudding

    Pour fruit and juice into a bowl. Add instant vanilla pudding and mix well. Stir in bananas. Spoon salad into dessert dishes. Refrigerate for 2 to 3 hours.

Optional: Add ½ cup miniature marshmallows.

STRAWBERRY-GINGER ALE SALAD

1 (3 oz.) pkg. strawberry jello
1 c. ginger ale, chilled
1 c. Birds Eye quick thaw
   strawberries, thawed
   and drained

Dissolve jello as package directs in 1 cup boiling water. Stir in 1 cup ginger ale. Refrigerate until partially thickened. Stir in well drained strawberries. (Optional: Add sliced bananas.) Mix well. Pour into a mold or square dish and chill until firm.

FROZEN CRANBERRY SALAD

1 (16 oz.) can whole
   cranberry sauce
1 (8 oz.) container Cool Whip

1 (15½ oz.) can crushed
   pineapple, drained

Combine, mix, and freeze. Serves 4 to 6.

This mixture could be poured into paper muffin cups setting inside muffin tins and frozen.

INSTANT SALAD

1 (24 oz.) ctn. cottage cheese
1 (3 oz.) pkg. strawberry jello

1 (8 oz.) ctn. Cool Whip
   topping

Combine drained cottage cheese with dry jello and mix well. Stir in Cool Whip. Refrigerate for 2 to 3 hours before serving.

Optional: Stir in sliced strawberries.

MYRTLE HULL'S CRANBERRY RELISH

1 lb. fresh cranberries
2 oranges, seeded, sliced or
   chopped

1 or 2 c. sugar (to taste)

Wash berries and oranges. Cook cranberries as package directs in boiling water until skins pop, about 1 minute. Drain well and pour into a bowl.

Chop oranges and rind and remove seeds. Pour into bowl and mix with cranberries. Add sugar to taste. Cover and refrigerate.

SHAMROCK JELLO SALAD

1 (3 oz.) pkg. lime jello   2 sliced bananas or chopped
1 pt. vanilla ice cream   apples

Mix jello with 1½ cups boiling water. Stir in ice cream. Chill until partially set. Stir in sliced bananas. Chill until firm. Serves 4.

LIME JELLO SALAD

1 (3 oz.) pkg. lime Jell-O   1 (15 oz.) can crushed
1 c. cottage cheese   pineapple, drained

Dissolve Jell-O in 1 cup boiling water. Stir in ½ cup cold water; chill until partially set. Stir in pineapple and cottage cheese. Refrigerate until firm. Serves 4.

WILLIE COPELAND'S CUCUMBER SALAD

2 cucumbers, sliced, peeled,
    and seeded

Heinz cider vinegar
1 sliced red onion

Combine; mix and chill. Serves 4.

Optional: Mix sliced cucumbers with sour cream instead of vinegar.

WATERGATE PISTACHIO SALAD

1 (20 oz.) can crushed
    pineapple (undrained)
1 (12 oz.) Cool Whip (or less)

1 (3½ oz.) pkg. instant
    pistachio pudding mix
    (dry)

Combine and mix all ingredients together. Chill 2 to 3 hours before serving.

Optional: Add chopped nuts or maraschino cherries, if desired. Serves 4 to 6.

ROGENE'S CHERRY BERRY SALAD

1 (6 oz.) pkg. cherry Jell-O   1 (15 oz.) can whole berry
1 (10 oz.) pkg. frozen   cranberry sauce
    strawberries

    Dissolve Jell-O as package directs in 2 cups boiling water, mixing well. Stir in undrained strawberries and whole berry cranberry sauce. Pour into 7x11 inch glass dish and refrigerate until set. Serves 8 to 10.

    Optional: Frost firm gelatin with sour cream.

PINEAPPLE BOATS

1 fresh pineapple   1 can tropical fruit salad,
2 Tbsp. shredded coconut   drained

    Cut fresh pineapple in half, leaves and all. Remove core and fruit, leaving ½ inch thick shell. Reserve pineapple.

    Fill with a can of drained tropical fruit, mixed with reserved pineapple. Sprinkle coconut over top. Serves 2.

JIM WORNALL'S
PEACH AND COTTAGE CHEESE SALAD

1 c. cottage cheese
2 maraschino cherries

1 (16 oz.) can peaches
   (halves or slices),
   drained

Place a scoop of cottage cheese on a lettuce leaf in center of a salad plate, surrounded by peaches. Place a maraschino cherry on top of cottage cheese as a garnish. (This is my husband's favorite salad.) Serves 2.

DEVILED EGGS

6 hard-boiled eggs, halved
Thousand Island salad
   dressing

Paprika

Mix egg yolks with a little dressing. Stuff into egg white shells. Sprinkle with paprika. Refrigerate. Serves 6.

CRABMEAT SALAD

1 c. crabmeat
1 c. pared, chopped apples

¼ to ½ c. mayonnaise

Combine, mix, and chill. Serve on lettuce leaf. Serves 4.

Optional: Serve salad in avocado cups. Cut avocado in half, remove seed, and fill hollow with crab salad.

RASPBERRY-APPLESAUCE SALAD

1 (3 oz.) pkg. raspberry Jell-
  O
1 c. applesauce

1 (10 oz.) pkg. frozen
  raspberries

Heat applesauce just to boiling. Stir in dry Jell-O and mix well. Stir in thawed raspberries. Pour into a mold or bowl and refrigerate until firm. Serves 4.

MANDARIN ORANGE WHIP

1 (3 oz.) box dry orange Jell-O
1 (12 oz.) Cool Whip

2 (11 oz.) cans mandarin oranges, drained

Mix together the dry Jell-O and Cool Whip. Stir in drained oranges and refrigerate for a couple of hours before serving. Serves 4.

SUMMER SPINACH SALAD

4 c. fresh spinach, washed and torn into pieces

12 fresh strawberries, sliced
1 c. green seedless grapes

Combine, toss, and serve with poppy seed dressing. Serves 4.

Variation: Substitute romaine lettuce for spinach.

WILMA DAVIS' CRAN-APPLE SALAD

1 (3 oz.) pkg. orange Jell-O
2 chopped apples

1 (16 oz.) can whole berry
   cranberry sauce

     Prepare orange Jell-O as package directs, using 1 cup boiling water. Stir until well dissolved. Cool. Add can whole berry cranberry sauce and 2 chopped apples. Mix well. Cover and refrigerate until firm. Serves 6.

STRAWBERRY SOUFFLE SALAD

1 (3 oz.) pkg. strawberry Jell-
   O gelatin

1 c. boiling water
1 c. mashed strawberries

     Stir until Jell-O is dissolved in the boiling water. Add mashed berries and mix. Refrigerate until mixture begins to thicken, then whip with an eggbeater or electric mixer to a very stiff froth.

     Serve in sherbet dishes or in any small bowls. Serves 4.

     Contains negligible fat grams.

MARTHA BRECKENRIDGE'S FRUIT SALAD

2 c. seedless grapes (red and green)

2 c. cubed cantaloupe
1 to 2 c. sliced strawberries

Combine, mix, and refrigerate until serving time. Serves 6.

JUDY MUELLER'S HONEY-LIME DRESSING

¼ c. fresh lime juice
⅛ c. honey

¼ tsp. Dijon mustard

Mix the 3 ingredients together. Cover and refrigerate! Serve chilled over lettuce or fruit salads. Yield: ⅓ cup. *Fat free!*

Note: Judy serves this dressing over a romaine and honeydew melon salad.

DORIS HANKS' TOMATO-ASPARAGUS SALAD

2 fresh tomatoes   1 head romaine lettuce
1 lb. fresh asparagus spears

Slice tomatoes. Cook fresh asparagus in boiling water for 5 to 6 minutes or until tender. Drain. Chill asparagus.

Line 4 salad plates with romaine lettuce leaves. Top with additional lettuce that had been torn in bite-size pieces. Arrange chilled asparagus spears and tomato slices over the lettuce. Serves 4. *Fat free!*

Optional: If desired, drizzle with fat-free Italian salad dressing.

DIETER'S SALAD DRESSING

1 (16 oz.) ctn. 1% lowfat,   1 (2 oz.) pkg. lowfat original
   small curd cottage   Ranch salad dressing
   cheese   mix
2 c. lowfat buttermilk

Combine the 3 ingredients in a bowl and mix well. Pour into a 1 quart covered container or jar and shake until blended. Keep refrigerated. Shake before using. Yield: 1 quart.

Contains 6 calories per 2 tablespoons.

Optional: The dressing can be poured into a blender and blended until smooth.

PAM'S TRIPLE ORANGE SALAD

1 (3 oz.) pkg. orange jello
1 pt. orange sherbet

1 (11 oz.) can mandarin
    oranges, drained

Dissolve jello as package directs. Don't add any cold water. Stir in sherbet, then oranges. Refrigerate until firm. Serves 4.

SAUTEED APPLES

4 to 6 apples, peeled, cored,
    and sliced

Flour
Melted margarine

Roll apples in flour, then saute in melted margarine until golden brown. (Optional: Sprinkle with sugar or cinnamon.) Serve with ham or roast pork. Serves 4.

COTTAGE CHEESE SALAD

1 (24 oz.) ctn. cottage   **1 to 2 chopped tomatoes**
    cheese, drained
2 to 3 chopped green onions
    (and tops)

    Combine cottage cheese, green onions, and tomatoes. Mix and serve chilled. Serves 4 to 6.

    Optional: Serve in large, red, hollowed-out tomatoes.

"If a recipe has more than 3 ingredients, it's not easy!"

Vegetables

EQUIVALENT CHART

3 tsp.	1 Tbsp.
2 Tbsp.	⅛ c.
4 Tbsp.	¼ c.
8 Tbsp.	½ c.
16 Tbsp.	1 c.
5 Tbsp. + 1 tsp.	⅓ c.
12 Tbsp.	¾ c.
4 oz.	½ c.
8 oz.	1 c.
16 oz.	1 lb.
1 oz.	2 Tbsp. fat or liquid
2 c.	1 pt.
2 pt.	1 qt.
1 qt.	4 c.
⅝ c.	½ c. + 2 Tbsp.
⅞ c.	¾ c. + 2 Tbsp.
1 jigger	1½ fl. oz. (3 Tbsp.)
8 to 10 egg whites	1 c.
12 to 14 egg yolks	1 c.
1 c. unwhipped cream	2 c. whipped
1 lb. shredded American cheese	4 c.
¼ lb. crumbled Bleu cheese	1 c.
1 lemon	3 Tbsp. juice
1 orange	⅓ c. juice
1 lb. unshelled walnuts	1½ to 1¾ c. shelled
2 c. fat	1 lb.
1 lb. butter	2 c. or 4 sticks
2 c. granulated sugar	1 lb.
3½-4 c. unsifted powdered sugar	1 lb.
2¼ c. packed brown sugar	1 lb.
4 c. sifted flour	1 lb.
4½ c. cake flour	1 lb.
3½ c. unsifted whole wheat flour	1 lb.
4 oz. (1 to 1¼ c.) uncooked macaroni	2¼ c. cooked
7 oz. spaghetti	4 c. cooked
4 oz. (1½ to 2 c.) uncooked noodles	2 c. cooked
28 saltine crackers	1 c. crumbs
4 slices bread	1 c. crumbs
14 square graham crackers	1 c. crumbs
22 vanilla wafers	1 c. crumbs

SUBSTITUTIONS FOR A MISSING INGREDIENT

1 square **chocolate** (1 ounce) = 3 or 4 tablespoons cocoa plus ½ tablespoon fat
1 tablespoon **cornstarch** (for thickening) = 2 tablespoons flour
1 cup sifted **all-purpose flour** = 1 cup plus 2 tablespoons sifted cake flour
1 cup sifted **cake flour** = 1 cup minus 2 tablespoons sifted all-purpose flour
1 teaspoon **baking powder** = ¼ teaspoon baking soda plus ½ teaspoon cream of tartar
1 cup **sour milk** = 1 cup sweet milk into which 1 tablespoon vinegar or lemon juice has been stirred
1 cup **sweet milk** = 1 cup sour milk or buttermilk plus ½ teaspoon baking soda
¾ cup **cracker crumbs** = 1 cup bread crumbs
1 cup **cream, sour, heavy** = ⅓ cup butter and ⅔ cup milk in any sour milk recipe
1 teaspoon **dried herbs** = 1 tablespoon fresh herbs
1 cup **whole milk** = ½ cup evaporated milk and ½ cup water or 1 cup reconstituted nonfat dry milk and 1 tablespoon butter
2 ounces **compressed yeast** = 3 (¼ ounce) packets of dry yeast
1 tablespoon **instant minced onion, rehydrated** = 1 small fresh onion
1 tablespoon **prepared mustard** = 1 teaspoon dry mustard
⅛ teaspoon **garlic powder** = 1 small pressed clove of garlic
1 lb. **whole dates** = 1½ cups, pitted and cut
3 medium **bananas** = 1 cup mashed
3 cups **dry corn flakes** = 1 cup crushed
10 **miniature marshmallows** = 1 large marshmallow

GENERAL OVEN CHART

Very slow oven	250° to 300°F.
Slow oven	300° to 325°F.
Moderate oven	325° to 375°F.
Medium hot oven	375° to 400°F.
Hot oven	400° to 450°F.
Very hot oven	450° to 500°F.

CONTENTS OF CANS

Of the different sizes of cans used by commercial canners, the most common are:

Size:	Average Contents
8 oz.	1 cup
Picnic	1¼ cups
No. 300	1¾ cups
No. 1 tall	2 cups
No. 303	2 cups
No. 2	2½ cups
No. 2½	3½ cups
No. 3	4 cups
No. 10	12 to 13 cups

VEGETABLES

❖   ❖   ❖

AUDREY'S GREEN BEANS

1 (16 oz.) can cut green beans   1 Tbsp. Lipton onion soup
1 tsp. olive oil   mix

    Combine the 3 ingredients in a saucepan. Mix and heat slowly for 20 to 30 minutes, stirring occasionally. Serves 4.

DILLED NEW POTATOES

24 small red-skinned   4 Tbsp. chopped fresh dill (or
   potatoes   dried dill weed)
3 Tbsp. lowfat margarine

    Boil potatoes until tender. Drain. Melt margarine. Stir in dill, then toss mixture with hot potatoes. Serve hot. Serves 6.

BARBARA WRIGHT'S LEMON BROCCOLI

1 (10 oz.) box frozen broccoli   **2 Tbsp. lowfat margarine**
1½ Tbsp. lemon juice

Prepare broccoli according to package directions. Drain.

Melt 2 tablespoons margarine and remove from heat. Stir in 1½ tablespoons lemon juice. Mix together, then pour over broccoli. Serves 4.

MINTED PEAS

1 (16 oz.) can green peas,   **1 Tbsp. lowfat margarine**
**   drained**   **⅓ c. mint jelly**

Drain peas, but reserve liquid. Cook liquid until it has reduced to ¼ cup. Stir in peas, margarine, and mint jelly. Heat thoroughly. Serves 4.

BROCCOLI RICE CASSEROLE

1 (10 oz.) box frozen   1 c. cooked rice
    chopped broccoli   1 small jar Cheez Whiz

Cook broccoli according to package directions. Cook rice according to package directions.

Combine broccoli, rice, and Cheez Whiz. Mix well. Pour into greased casserole dish and bake at 350°F. for 20 to 30 minutes. Serves 6.

CAVIAR POTATOES

4 to 6 baking potatoes   1 (8 oz.) ctn. sour cream
1 jar caviar

Bake potatoes at 400°F. for an hour or until done.

Split potatoes and serve with a dollop of sour cream. Top with a spoonful of caviar. Serves 4 to 6.

ONION RICE CASSEROLE

1 (10¾ oz.) can French onion
   soup

1 c. water
1 c. rice (not instant)

    Combine soup, rice, and water. Mix well and cook in a covered saucepan over medium heat for 25 minutes or until the rice is tender. Fluff with a fork. Serves 4.

CABBAGE CASSEROLE

1 head cabbage, washed and
   cooked
1 (10¾ oz.) can cream of
   chicken soup

1 c. shredded Cheddar
   Cheese

    In a buttered casserole dish, make alternate layers of cabbage, soup, and cheese. Repeat layers. Bake at 350°F. for 30 minutes. Serves 4 to 6.

MAXINE McNEIL'S ORANGE CARROTS

1 Tbsp. butter or margarine	1 (15 oz.) can sliced carrots,
1 Tbsp. orange marmalade	drained

Combine butter and marmalade in a small saucepan and heat until melted, stirring often. Add drained carrots; stir and heat until hot and glazed. Serves 4.

MYRTLE HULL'S GREEN BEAN CASSEROLE

1 (16 oz.) can green beans, drained	1 small can French fried onion rings
1 (10 oz.) can mushroom soup	

Combine beans, soup, and ½ can onion rings. Mix well. Pour into a greased baking dish and bake at 350°F. for 25 minutes. Top with remaining onion rings and bake 10 minutes longer. Serves 4 to 6.

JULIE'S SCALLOPED ONIONS

6 onions, peeled and sliced   **1 small box Velveeta cheese**
3 c. crushed potato chips

     Boil onions until limp and transparent. Butter a casserole dish and layer onions alternately with cheese and potato chips. Repeat layers 1 to 2 times. Bake 20 minutes at 350°F. (This is my favorite!) Serves 6.

ETHEL JONES' BROCCOLI PARMESAN

1 (10 oz.) pkg. frozen   **Butter Buds sprinkles**
   broccoli, thawed   **Nonfat Parmesan cheese**

     Cook broccoli as package directs. Drain. Sprinkle generously with Butter Buds and Parmesan cheese. Serves 4. *Fat free!*

CHARLOTTE'S ONION ROASTED POTATOES

2 lb. potatoes   ⅓ c. olive oil
1 pkg. Lipton dry onion soup
   mix

   Wash and peel potatoes. Cut into chunks. Pour all ingredients into a large plastic bag, close bag, and shake until potatoes are coated, or potatoes can be mixed in a bowl. Empty potatoes into a greased 9x13 inch pan. (Discard bag.) Bake at 450°F. for 40 minutes or until tender and golden brown, *stirring occasionally.* Serves 4 to 6.

BAKED CORN-ON-THE-COB

6 ears of corn   Lemon pepper
Lowfat margarine

   Husk fresh corn, remove silk, wash, and dry with paper towels.

   Spread margarine on corn, sprinkle with lemon pepper, and wrap in foil. Bake at 325°F. for 30 minutes. Serves 6.

GREEN BEANS ALMONDINE

1 or 2 (10 oz.) pkg. frozen   ⅓ c. slivered almonds
   green beans   3 Tbsp. melted margarine

    Heat beans according to package directions. Drain well. In a small saucepan, saute almonds in melted margarine. Stir almonds and margarine into green beans. Serves 4 to 6.

CORN FRITTERS

Pancake mix   Margarine
1 can whole kernel corn

    Prepare pancake mix according to package directions. Stir corn into pancake batter. Fry cakes in melted hot margarine as you would fry pancakes.

GAY HERNDON'S POTATO CASSEROLE

5 potatoes, peeled and sliced
1 (10¾ oz.) can cream of
   mushroom soup

1 c. grated Cheddar cheese

    Place a layer of sliced potatoes in a greased casserole dish. Pour soup, that has been diluted with water, over the potatoes. Mix well. Bake for 45 minutes at 400°F., covered. Uncover; top with cheese and bake for 15 minutes longer.

    Optional: Add onions before baking.

SPINACH WITH BOILED EGGS

2 (16 oz.) cans spinach
1 Tbsp. vinegar

2 eggs, hard-boiled

    Cook spinach, heating thoroughly. Drain. Stir in vinegar. Boil 2 eggs; cool and slice. Pour spinach into a bowl and garnish with sliced, hard-boiled eggs.

BOILED NEW POTATOES

3 lb. small new potatoes   6 Tbsp. minced parsley
¾ c. melted margarine

    Cook 3 pounds small new potatoes, that have been washed, in 5 cups boiling water until tender; drain. Sprinkle with melted margarine and minced parsley. Serve hot.

PIZZA POTATOES

1 box scalloped potatoes   1 c. pepperoni slices
1 c. shredded Mozzarella
  cheese

    Prepare potatoes according to package directions and pour into a greased casserole dish. Spread cheese over potatoes, then arrange pepperoni slices over cheese. Bake at 400°F. for 30 to 35 minutes. Serves 6.

RITZY CARROT CASSEROLE

2 (16 oz.) cans carrots,
  drained and heated

1 small jar Cheez Whiz,
  melted
1 tube crushed Ritz crackers

Drain heated carrots and pour them into a greased baking dish. Top with melted Cheez Whiz. Spread crushed Ritz crackers over carrots. Bake at 300°F. until golden brown.

CREAMED CORN

1 large box frozen whole
  kernel corn

8 oz. cream cheese, softened
Lemon pepper to taste

Cook corn according to package directions; drain. Stir cream cheese into hot corn; stir until melted and well heated. Season to taste with lemon pepper.

SPEEDY BAKED BEANS

3 (16 oz.) cans pork and
    beans
5 to 6 Tbsp. chili sauce

4 Tbsp. brown sugar

    Mix the beans, chili sauce, and sugar. Bake in a greased casserole dish, uncovered, for about an hour at 325°F.

    Optional: If desired, lay 3 or 4 strips of bacon on top of beans before baking.

VELMA STEWART'S STUFFED CELERY

4 stalks celery, washed and
    strings removed
1 (8 oz.) pkg. cream cheese,
    softened

16 pimento stuffed green
    olives, sliced (or
    paprika)

    Cut celery into 2 inch lengths. Stuff with cream cheese. Dot with green olive slices (or sprinkle with paprika). Serves 6 to 8.

NEW YEAR'S BLACK-EYED PEAS

1 (16 oz.) can black-eyed
   peas, drained

8 slices pepperoni, chopped
2 Tbsp. chopped onion

Combine peas, pepperoni, and onion. Heat thoroughly. Serves 4.

GREEN PEAS DELUXE

2 (10 oz.) pkg. frozen green
   peas
1 (10¾ oz.) can cream of
   mushroom soup

1 small can water chestnuts,
   chopped

Prepare green peas according to package directions. Drain. Stir in water chestnuts and soup. Heat well in a saucepan or pour into a greased baking dish and bake for 25 minutes at 350°F. Serves 6 to 8.

HOMINY CASSEROLE

2 (15½ oz.) cans yellow
   hominy, drained

1 c. shredded Cheddar
   cheese
1 small chopped onion

    Place alternate layers of hominy, onions, and cheese in a greased baking dish. Repeat layers. Bake for 30 minutes at 350°F. Serves 6.

VEGETABLE CHRISTMAS TREE

Cauliflower
Broccoli

Cherry tomatoes

    Build the tree on a large tray or platter. Make the tree trunk out of the broccoli stem. Build the first row of the tree with cauliflowerets, next row with tomatoes, etc., alternating rows. Decrease size of each row. Outline tree with broccoli flowerets. Serve with dip of choice. Serves 8 to 10.

BRAM'S BAKED POTATOES
WITH LEMON PEPPER

4 to 6 Idaho potatoes　　　　**Lemon pepper to taste**
Butter or margarine

　　Scrub and prick potatoes. Place in center of oven and bake about 1 hour at 375°F. Let set 10 minutes, then cut lengthwise. Top with margarine. Sprinkle generously with lemon pepper. Serves 4 to 6.

　　Note: If in a hurry, you can microwave potatoes about 5 minutes for 1 and 12 to 14 minutes for 4.

MEN'S FAVORITE GREEN BEANS

2 (16 oz.) cans green beans,　　**Pimiento, chopped fine**
**　drained**　　　　　　　　　　**1 (8 oz.) jar Kraft Cheez Whiz**

　　Combine, mix and heat thoroughly. Serves 6.

　　Mrs. Manning, who gave me the recipe, assured me that men love this!

CHEEZY GREEN PEAS

1 (16 oz.) can green peas   1 small jar Kraft Cheez Whiz
3 Tbsp. chopped onion

Combine peas, onions, and cheese. Mix well and heat thoroughly. (Can be heated in microwave or baked 15 minutes at 325°F.) Serves 4.

Note: For a different taste, try jalapeno flavored Cheez Whiz. Very good!

FRIED ONION RINGS

2 onions, sliced   Pancake mix
Enough water or milk to
    make a batter

Separate sliced onions into rings. Mix together the pancake mix and water (or milk if directions call for it). Dip onion rings into batter. Fry in deep oil until golden brown. Drain on paper towels. Serves 2 to 4.

PECAN RICE PILAF

1 pkg. wild rice
3 Tbsp. margarine

½ c. pecan halves

Saute pecan halves in melted margarine. Prepare wild rice according to package directions. Stir pecans into rice. Serve hot with chicken.

MOTHER'S FRIED GREEN TOMATOES

2 to 3 green tomatoes, sliced
½ c. flour or corn meal

1 beaten egg

Dip tomato slices in flour and fry in oil.

Or, dip tomato slices in a beaten egg, then dip in flour on both sides. Fry in vegetable oil.

Or, optional: Dip tomato slices in corn meal and fry. Serves 4.

LILA OBERCROM'S GREEN BEANS AND BACON

2 lb. fresh green beans (or canned)

6 slices bacon, chopped
1 c. onion, chopped

Fry bacon until crisp, then remove to drain on paper towels. Cook onions in bacon fat until slightly wilted, then stir in beans. Cook 1 minute. Add 1 tablespoon water; cover and cook 3 minutes. Uncover and cook 3 to 5 minutes longer or until hot. Add crisp bacon just before serving. Serves 6.

PEAS AND CARROTS

1 (16 oz.) can green peas
1 (16 oz.) can chopped or sliced carrots, drained

1 Tbsp. margarine

Combine, mix, and heat thoroughly. Serves 6 to 8.

CAULIFLOWER AND GREEN PEAS

1 (10 oz.) pkg. frozen
   cauliflower
1 (16 oz.) can LeSueur green
   peas

2 Tbsp. lowfat margarine or
   prepared Butter Buds

Prepare cauliflower as package directs. Drain. Stir in drained green peas and margarine. Heat thoroughly, stirring occasionally. Serves 6.

RICE PILAF

2 c. cooked rice
⅓ c. raisins or chopped dates

¼ c. slivered almonds,
   toasted

Combine and mix. Serve hot. Great with chicken. Serves 4.

ETHEL JONES' STEAMED ASPARAGUS

1 lb. fresh asparagus   Butter Buds sprinkles
Juice of 1 lemon

    Wash asparagus. Place on a vegetable steamer rack over boiling water. Cover and steam about 6 minutes or until tender. Sprinkle with lemon juice and Butter Buds. Serves 4. *Fat free!*

JUDY MUELLER'S MASHED POTATOES

4 or 5 potatoes, peeled and   Butter Buds sprinkles
   sliced   Evaporated skim milk

    Boil potatoes until tender and drain. Generously sprinkle Butter Buds sprinkles over potatoes and mix well. Cover with a lid and let set for 3 minutes. Mash potatoes with desired amount of evaporated skim milk. Serves 4.

JESSICA WORNALL'S SOUTHWESTERN BAKED POTATOES

4 baking potatoes
1 (8 oz.) jar thick and chunky salsa

4 Tbsp. nonfat Cheddar cheese, shredded

Wash potatoes and prick their skins several times. Bake for 1 hour or until tender at 400°F. (Do *not* wrap potatoes in foil.)

Split tops of potatoes. Spoon desired amount of salsa into each. Top with shredded Cheddar cheese. Serves 4.

Contains 1 fat gram per potato.

"If a recipe has more than 3 ingredients, it's not easy!"

Notes

Main Dishes

MEAT ROASTING GUIDE

Cut	Weight Pounds	Approx. Time (Hours) (325° oven)	Internal Temperature
BEEF			
Standing rib roast			
(10 inch) ribs	4	1¾	140° (rare)
(If using shorter cut (8-inch)		2	160° (medium)
ribs, allow 30 min. longer)		2½	170° (well done)
	8	2½	140° (rare)
		3	160° (medium)
		4½	170° (well done)
Rolled ribs	4	2	140° (rare)
		2½	160° (medium)
		3	170° (well done)
	6	3	140° (rare)
		3¼	160° (medium)
		4	170° (well done)
Rolled rump	5	2¼	140° (rare)
(Roast only if high quality.	3	160° (medium)	
Otherwise, braise.)		3¼	170° (well done)
Sirloin tip	3	1½	140° (rare)
(Roast only if high quality.		2	160° (medium)
Otherwise, braise.)		2¼	170° (well done)
LAMB			
Leg	6	3	175° (medium)
		3½	180° (well done)
	8	4	175° (medium)
		4½	180° (well done)
VEAL			
Leg (piece)	5	2½ to 3	170° (well done)
Shoulder	6	3½	170° (well done)
Rolled shoulder	3 to 5	3 to 3½	170° (well done)

POULTRY ROASTING GUIDE

Type of Poultry	Ready-To- Cook Weight	Oven Temperature	Approx. Total Roasting Time
TURKEY	6 to 8 lb.	325°	2½ to 3 hr.
	8 to 12 lb.	325°	3 to 3½ hr.
	12 to 16 lb.	325°	3½ to 4 hr.
	16 to 20 lb.	325°	4 to 4½ hr.
	20 to 24 lb.	300°	5 to 6 hr.
CHICKEN	2 to 2½ lb.	400°	1 to 1½ hr.
(Unstuffed)	2½ to 4 lb.	400°	1½ to 2½ hr.
	4 to 8 lb.	325°	3 to 5 hr.
DUCK	3 to 5 lb.	325°	2½ to 3 hr.
(Unstuffed)			

NOTE: Small chickens are roasted at 400° so that they brown well in the short cooking time. They may also be done at 325° but will take longer and will not be as brown. Increase cooking time 15 to 20 minutes for stuffed chicken and duck.

MAIN DISHES

PEPSI HAM

1 (10 to 12 lb.) cooked
   boneless ham

Whole cloves
2 c. Pepsi-Cola

     Score a cooked boneless ham. Stud with whole cloves. Place ham in a roaster. Pour 1 cup Pepsi over it. Cover tightly with lid or foil. Bake 2 hours at 325°F. Baste occasionally with the second cup of Pepsi. Serves 20.

ROAST TURKEY

Turkey (12 to 16 lb.)
Salt

Melted margarine

     Rinse turkey and pat dry with paper towels after removing giblets and neck; salt. Place turkey, breast side up, on rack in roasting pan. Baste occasionally with melted margarine. Put a tent of foil over the turkey. Roast at 325°F. for 3½ to 5 hours for 12 to 16 pound turkey. Remove foil during the last ½ hour to brown. Turkey is done when you can "shake its leg" and juices run clear (no pink). Serves 20 to 24.

MUSHROOM STEAK

1 round steak (2 lb.)
1 (10¾ oz.) can mushroom
soup

1 small can sliced
mushrooms, drained

Place a round steak in a 9x13 inch pan lined with foil. Pour 1 can mushroom soup over steak and top with 1 small can drained, sliced mushrooms. Cover with foil. Bake 1 hour or until tender at 350°F. Serves 4 to 6.

MOTHER'S POT ROAST WITH VEGETABLES

1 beef roast (3 to 4 lb.)
2 onions

4 potatoes, peeled

Grease a heavy skillet or Dutch oven. Lay roast on it and sear or brown meat on medium high heat on all sides.

Pour 2 inches of water around the meat; cover and heat on low for several hours or until tender. Season to taste.

Add quartered potatoes and onion to the pot about 1 hour before roast is done. Serves 8.

HAMBURGER STROGANOFF

1 lb. hamburger or ground   1 pkg. noodles
    round
2 (10¾ oz.) cans cream of
    mushroom soup

Brown hamburger; drain. Stir soups into the crumbled hamburger and mix well. Cook for 10 minutes, or until thoroughly heated; stir often. Boil noodles according to package directions; drain. Serve hamburger mixture over noodles.

Optional: Brown a chopped onion with hamburger.

BEEF KABOBS

Sirloin tips, cut into bite-size   Green peppers, cubed
    pieces   Cherry tomatoes

Alternate beef, peppers, and cherry tomatoes on long skewers. (If desired, brush with melted margarine or barbecue sauce.) Place on a grill 4 to 5 inches above hot coals. Turn occasionally. Cook until meat is brown to desired doneness.

SOLE ELEGANTE

1 (4 count) pkg. frozen sole   ½ c. Parmesan cheese
    fillets
1 can cream of shrimp soup

    Arrange fish in a greased baking dish. Spread soup over fish, then sprinkle Parmesan cheese on top. Bake for 25 minutes at 425°F. Serves 4.

CAROLE MARIE'S LEMON RUMP ROAST

1 (2 to 3 lb.) rump roast   1 c. lemon juice
½ tsp. lemon pepper

    Trim all visible fat from meat. Place rump roast in a Pyrex dish. Prick top of roast with a fork. Pour lemon juice over roast. Rub juice into the meat. Cover and refrigerate 6 hours or overnight. Turn 2 to 3 times. Drain off juice; sprinkle meat with lemon pepper. Place in a baking dish and roast at 325°F. for about 2 hours.

VELMA STEWART'S CELERY STEAK

Round steak
1 can cream of celery soup

Dash of onion salt or paprika

Place steak in a greased 9x13 inch pan. Spread soup over it. Sprinkle with onion salt. Cover pan with foil. Bake for 1 hour, or until tender, at 350°F. Baste once or twice with soup if you think of it.

MERLE'S CORNISH HEN A LA ORANGE

4 Cornish hens, rinsed and
  dried
2 to 3 Tbsp. melted
  margarine

1 (10 oz.) jar orange
  marmalade

Place hens in a greased large baking pan. Mix together melted margarine and orange marmalade; set aside. Bake hens for 30 minutes at 350°F. Pour orange mixture over them and bake for 1 hour longer, basting several times.

This is good served with wild rice.

PARTY CHICKEN

1 pkg. dried beef, sliced
4 chicken breasts, boned,
    skinned, and halved

2 (10¾ oz.) cans mushroom
    soup

Spread dried beef slices in bottom of a greased baking dish. Lay chicken over beef. Pour mushroom soup over chicken. Refrigerate 3 hours. Bake at 275° for 2½ hours or until chicken is tender. Serves 4.

Note: Sometimes I chop the dried beef, mix it with the soup, and pour it over the chicken before baking. Sometimes I do *not* refrigerate this before baking. It's great either way. I serve this with wild rice, a cranberry-cherry Jell-O salad, and green beans.

JANE WISS' CHICKEN AND DUMPLINGS

1 stewing chicken
Salted water

1 pkg. flour tortillas, cubed
    or cut into squares

Boil chicken until tender. Remove from broth and debone. Discard bones. Return chicken meat to broth. Bring to a boil. Drop tortilla cubes into broth. Reduce heat and cook on low for 10 minutes. The tortilla cubes will puff up like dumplings. Serves 4.

JIM WORNALL'S APPLE JACK CHICKEN

6 chicken breasts, skinned
   and boned
2 or 3 Jonathan apples,
   sliced thin

6 slices Monterey Jack
   cheese

Preheat oven to 350°F. Place chicken in a greased 9x13 inch pan. Bake 30 minutes. Turn chicken over. Lay apple slices over each breast and bake 15 minutes. Remove from oven and top each piece with a slice of cheese. Bake 15 minutes longer or until cheese melts and chicken is tender. Serves 6.

LOIS DAVIS' ORANGE CHICKEN

1 chicken, cut in serving
   pieces
1 (12 oz.) can orange soda

¼ c. soy sauce

Place chicken pieces in a foil-lined 9x13 inch pan that has been sprayed with Pam.

Mix together the orange soda and soy sauce, then pour it over the chicken. Bake at 325°F. for 1 hour or until chicken is tender. Baste chicken occasionally as it bakes. Serves 4.

CHICKEN PARMESAN

**4 to 6 chicken breasts,
halved, boned, and
skinned**

**⅓ c. melted margarine
Parmesan cheese**

Roll chicken in melted margarine first and then in Parmesan cheese until well-coated. Place chicken in a greased baking pan and drizzle a little extra margarine over each piece. Bake at 350°F. for 45 to 50 minutes or until tender. Serves 4 to 6.

ARTICHOKE CHICKEN

**8 half chicken breasts,
skinned and boned
2 (4 oz.) jars marinated
artichoke hearts**

8 slices Swiss cheese

Between 2 pieces of waxed paper, flatten chicken to uniform thickness. Brown chicken breasts on both sides in a well-greased skillet. Arrange them in a single layer in a greased 9x13 inch pan.

Drain artichoke hearts and chop coarsely. Spread on top of chicken. Lay Swiss cheese over all and bake at 350°F. for 20 to 30 minutes until chicken is tender and cheese melts. Serves 4 to 8.

Good with rice, green peas, and sliced tomato salad.

SAUSAGE-RICE CASSEROLE

1 lb. sausage (I prefer R.B.
   Rice's hot sausage)

3 c. cooked rice
1 (10¾ oz.) can mushroom
   soup

Fry sausage; crumble and drain.

Combine and mix sausage, 3 cups cooked rice, and 1 can mushroom soup together. Pour into a greased casserole dish and bake at 350°F. for 30 minutes. Serves 4.

RITZY BAKED CHICKEN

4 chicken breasts, skinned,
   boned, and halved

1 c. sour cream
1 c. crushed Ritz crackers

Roll boneless, skinned chicken breasts in sour cream, then in crushed Ritz crackers. Bake at 350°F. for 1 hour or until tender.

Serve with rice, if desired. Serves 4.

BETTY'S QUESADILLAS

10 flour tortillas
1 small chopped onion

1 to 1½ c. shredded Cheddar
cheese

Place desired amount of cheese and onion in center of a flour tortilla. Roll up and secure with wooden picks. Fry in melted margarine on both sides until golden brown. Serves 4 to 5.

BOILED BRISKET

3 to 4 lb. beef brisket
1 onion, quartered

2 to 3 celery stalks and tops,
cut in 2 inch pieces

Place brisket in a pot with enough water to cover the meat. Add 1 quartered onion and celery tops and pieces. Cover with tight lid and simmer for 3 to 4 hours or until the meat is tender.

Serve with horseradish sauce, if desired. Serves 8 to 10.

BAKED CUBE STEAKS

4 to 6 cube steaks   **Flour**
2 c. water

Flour cube steaks and brown in greased skillet. Add 2 cups water and bake, covered, about 2 hours at 350°F. or until tender. Serves 4 to 6.

SPANISH MEATLOAF

1 lb. hamburger   **1 egg, beaten**
1 (16 oz.) can Spanish rice,
    drained

Combine and mix well. Pour into a greased loaf pan. Bake about 1 hour at 350°F. Drain off excess liquid. Serves 4 to 6.

Optional: May add 1 small chopped onion before baking.

MUSHROOM-ONION ROAST

1 chuck roast (3 to 4 lb.)   ½ pkg. dry soup mix
1 (10¾ oz.) can mushroom
   soup

    Brown or sear meat on all sides. (This step can be omitted, but the roast tastes better if it is seared.)

    Place roast on 2 to 3 thicknesses of foil. Spread soup over meat, then sprinkle with onion soup mix. Wrap roast tightly. Place in pan and bake at 325°F. for 3 to 4 hours or until done. Serves 8 to 12.

BROILED FISH FILLETS

4 (5 to 7 oz.) fish filets (¾   ⅓ c. mayonnaise
   inch thick)   3 Tbsp. Parmesan cheese

    Preheat broiler. Spread mayonnaise over each filet. Sprinkle cheese on top of each. Place in a broiler pan and broil 4 to 6 inches away from heat for 5 to 8 minutes, or until fish flakes easily when tested with a fork. Serves 4.

CHIPPER CHICKEN

1 (3 lb.) chicken, cut in   1 pkg. potato chips, crushed
    serving pieces   1 stick margarine, melted

      Dip chicken in melted margarine, then roll in crushed potato chips. Bake in a greased 9x13 inch pan for 1 hour, or until tender, at 350°F. Serves 4.

CHINESE TUNA BAKE

1 to 2 (6 oz.) cans tuna, well   1 (3 oz.) can Chinese fried
    drained   noodles
1 (10¾ oz.) can cream of
    celery soup

      In a bowl, combine tuna, soup, and half can of fried Chinese noodles. Mix well and pour into a greased casserole dish. Bake at 350° for 25 minutes. Remove from oven and top with remaining noodles. Bake for 10 minutes longer. Serves 4.

CREAMED TUNA

1 (6 oz.) can tuna fish,   **½ can milk**
    drained
1 (10¾ oz.) can cream of
    mushroom soup

Combine, mix, and heat well. Serve over rice, roast, noodles, or in patty shells. Serves 2.

Optional: Add ½ cup green peas to the creamed tuna.

NANCY McDONALD'S SOY BRISKET

1 (3 to 4 lb.) brisket   **Soy sauce**
Dash of garlic powder
    (optional)

Poke holes in brisket. Rub soy sauce in it until brisket turns brown. Bake, covered (with foil), at 250°F. for 6 to 8 hours. Sprinkle with garlic powder. Bake until tender. Serves 6 to 12.

ONION ROAST

1 rump or chuck roast (3 lb.)   **1 pkg. Lipton dry onion soup**
Dash of garlic powder   **mix**

Place a beef roast on a large sheet of foil. Sprinkle 1 package of Lipton onion soup mix over the meat. Sprinkle roast with a dash of garlic powder. Seal foil.

Place in large pan and bake 3 hours at 300°F. or until tender (or bake at 200°F. for 8 to 9 hours, depending on the size of the roast). Serves 6 to 10.

BARBECUED PORK CHOPS

4 to 6 pork chops   **1 to 2 c. Coca-Cola**
1 c. catsup

Brown pork chops in greased skillet. Pour Coke and catsup over chops. Cover with lid or foil and simmer about 1½ hours or until tender. Serves 4 to 6.

HUSBAND'S FAVORITE FLANK STEAK

1 (2 lb.) beef flank steak   ⅓ c. Worcestershire sauce
⅓ c. soy sauce

Score flank steak with a sharp knife and place in a Pyrex dish. Combine soy sauce and Worcestershire sauce and pour marinade over steak. Marinate steak in the refrigerator for 2 to 4 hours. Turn steak several times.

Remove steak from marinade and broil or grill steak to desired doneness. Turn with tongs and broil other side. Let set 10 minutes before slicing. Slice across the grain, diagonally, into thin strips. Serves 4 to 6.

MARY ALICE LAWRENCE'S FRIED CATFISH

Catfish   Corn meal
Vegetable oil

Dip catfish in corn meal and slowly fry on low heat in a little vegetable oil until golden on both sides.

MOTHER'S SALMON PATTIES

1 (7½ oz.) can pink salmon,
   rinsed and drained

1 beaten egg
1 c. cracker crumbs

     Combine salmon, egg, and crumbs. Mix well. Shape into patties and fry on both sides. Serves 4.

ONION CHICKEN

4 to 6 chicken breasts,
   skinned and boned
1 pkg. dry onion soup mix

1½ Tbsp. lowfat margarine,
   melted

     Trim off all visible fat. Place chicken breasts (or any preferred pieces) in a single layer in a shallow baking dish, sprayed with Pam, then sprinkle onion soup mix over it. Dribble melted margarine over chicken. Cover and bake at 350°F. for 1 hour. Serves 4 to 6.

LOIS ROHM'S CRISP CHICKEN

4 chicken breasts, split,   **2 egg whites, beaten**
** skinned, and boned**   **Crushed corn flakes**

Dip chicken in beaten egg whites, then roll in crushed corn flakes until well-coated. Spray a baking sheet with Pam cooking spray, then place chicken on it and bake for about an hour at 350°F. Serves 4.

JOANN LOWE'S HADDOCK FILETS

4 haddock filets   **1 Tbsp. olive oil**
2 Tbsp. lemon juice

Mix lemon juice and olive oil together; pour into skillet and heat. Place filets in pan and saute until brown on each side, about 5 minutes. Serves 4.

JUDY'S ORANGE-ONION CHICKEN

4 chicken breast halves,   1 c. orange juice
  skinned and boned   1 pkg. Lipton onion soup mix

Trim off any visible fat on the chicken. Spray a 9x13 inch pan with Pam cooking spray, then arrange chicken pieces in the pan. Pour orange juice over chicken, then sprinkle with onion soup mix.

Bake 30 minutes at 350°F. Turn chicken, then bake 30 minutes longer or until tender. Serves 4.

DONNA SPENCER'S LEMON PEPPER CHICKEN

4 to 6 chicken breast halves,   Soy sauce
  skinned   Lemon pepper to taste

Arrange chicken breasts in a greased 9x13 inch pan. Sprinkle liberally with soy sauce, then with lemon pepper.

Bake at 350°F. for 1 hour or until tender. Serves 4 to 6.

JUDY McDONALD HUTCHINSON'S
HAM AND RED-EYE GRAVY

4 slices country ham   **Strong black coffee**
Hot sauce

Fry ham slices in heavy skillet, turning frequently. Remove ham slices. Add coffee to skillet (in the amount of gravy desired). Simmer, stir, and scrape. Add hot sauce to taste. Serve with ham. Serves 4.

Judy was my college roommate during my senior year and she gave me this recipe.

CHILI CASSEROLE

2 (16 oz.) cans chili con carne   **1 pkg. corn chips (or Fritos)**
1 c. Cheddar cheese,
    shredded

Place alternate layers of chili and corn chips in a greased casserole dish. Top with cheese. Cover. Bake at 350°F. for 30 minutes. Serves 6 to 8.

COCA-COLA BARBEQUED CHICKEN

4 to 6 chicken breasts or any   ½ bottle catsup
   favorite chicken part   1 (12 oz.) Coca-Cola

    Skin, bone, and split chicken breasts. Place chicken in large greased skillet. Pour Cocoa-Cola and catsup over chicken. Cover; cook about 1 hour until tender. (Check at 30 to 45 minutes for doneness.) Serves 4 to 6.

BREAKFAST CASSEROLE

2½ c. shredded Cheddar   1 c. whipping cream
   cheese
6 eggs

    In a buttered 10x6 inch baking dish, make a layer of 1½ cups cheese. Carefully break 6 eggs over cheese. Pierce each egg yolk. Sprinkle 1 cup shredded cheese over eggs. Pour cream over the casserole. Bake at 350°F. for 15 to 20 minutes.

    Great served with bacon and toast! Serves 6.

VELMA STEWART'S RUSSIAN CHICKEN SAUCE

Sauce:

1 (8 oz.) bottle Russian salad   1 pkg. dry onion soup mix
    dressing   (Lipton)
1 (8 oz.) jar apricot preserves

Sauce: Combine Russian dressing, dry soup mix, and apricot preserves. Mix well. Pour over 6 chicken breasts in a buttered 9x13 inch dish. Bake 2 hours at 300°F. Serves 6.

HOBO DINNER

1 lb. hamburger   4 potatoes
4 onion slices

Shape hamburger into patties. Slice potatoes ½ inch thick. Place patties on square of foil. Top with potato slices (2 to 3), then a slice of onion. Season to taste. Fold tightly; place in pan and bake 45 minutes at 350°F. Serves 4.

CROWN ROAST PORK

6 to 8 lb. (20 ribs) pork loin   **Crab apples (small)**
Parsley

Ask your butcher to make the crown from 2 strips of pork loin containing about 20 ribs. Remove backbone. Season to taste.

Place roast in roasting pan, bone ends up. Wrap bone ends in foil. Roast, uncovered, at 325°F. for 2 to 3 hours, or until well done and tender.

To serve, replace foil wraps with crab apples or paper frills. Garnish platter with parsley. Serves 10.

MOCK FILLET MIGNON

1 to 2 lb. ground round steak   **½ pkg. dry onion soup mix**
Bacon   **(Lipton)**

Combine ground round and onion soup mix. Shape into thick patties. Wrap a slice of bacon around each and secure with wooden picks. Place in 9x13 inch oven dish and bake at 450°F. for 15 to 20 minutes or broil on each side.

Good with sauteed mushrooms, baked potatoes, lettuce and tomato salad, and cheesecake with blueberries.

BUTTERMILK BAKED ROAST

1 (3 to 5 lb.) roast beef (rump,   1 pkg. dry onion soup mix
    chuck, etc.)   ½ c. buttermilk

Trim off all visible fat. Place roast on foil which is lying on a cookie sheet. Sprinkle soup mix over meat, then drizzle buttermilk over meat. Wrap up foil and bake at 250°F. for 5 hours or to desired doneness. Drain well. Serves 12 to 16.

Optional: Place meat on a rack in a roasting pan. Cover tightly with foil and bake at 250°F. for 5 hours.

ERNIE MASSEY'S ITALIAN CHICKEN

4 to 6 chicken breasts,   1 (8 oz.) bottle Italian salad
    skinned, boned, and   dressing
    halved
Flour

Remove any fat from chicken. Roll chicken breasts (or thighs) in flour. Place in a greased 9x13 inch pan. Pour lowfat Italian dressing over chicken. Cover and bake for an hour or until tender at 350°F. Remove cover and bake until golden brown. Could be prepared in crock pot on LOW. Serves 4 to 6.

BEV WEST'S CRANBERRY SAUCE
FOR CHICKEN

1 (16 oz.) can whole berry
    cranberry sauce
1 pkg. onion soup mix

1 (8 oz.) bottle lowfat French
    dressing

Cranberry Sauce: Combine the 3 ingredients in a bowl and mix until well-blended. Refrigerate, covered, until ready to use. Yield: 3 cups.

To prepare chicken, place 8 boneless, skinless chicken breast halves in an oblong Pyrex glass dish and pour Cranberry Sauce evenly over chicken. Cover and marinate overnight in the refrigerator. The next day, bake at 350°F. for 1 hour or until tender. Serves 8.

Note: This recipe sounds awful, but tastes delicious! It will surprise you!

IRMA MOUTTET'S SUNDAY CHICKEN

4 chicken breast halves
1 (10¾ oz.) can mushroom
    soup

1½ c. shredded Cheddar
    cheese

Skin and bone chicken, then place it in a greased 9x13 inch pan and bake for ½ hour at 350°F.

Remove from oven and spread soup over chicken. Top with cheese. Bake ½ hour longer (more or less). Serves 4.

CORY RIGGS' BAR-B-QUE BEEF

1 lb. ground sirloin or
  hamburger
½ c. brown sugar

16 oz. bar-b-que sauce (your
  choice)

Brown, crumble, and drain the meat. Stir in brown sugar and bar-b-que sauce. Cover and simmer for 15 minutes, stirring often.

Spoon onto heated hamburger buns. Serves 4 to 6.

SPEEDY SPAGHETTI

1 lb. pkg. spaghetti
1 lb. hamburger
1 (32 oz.) jar Ragu chunky
  garden style spaghetti
  sauce (with extra
  tomatoes, garlic, and
  onions)

Prepare spaghetti according to package directions. Brown meat; crumble and drain. Stir spaghetti sauce into the meat and heat thoroughly. Pour drained spaghetti into a large platter and spread meat sauce over it. Or combine spaghetti and meat sauce and mix thoroughly. Serves 4.

Optional: Top with 1 cup shredded Cheddar cheese and heat at 350° until cheese is melted.

CHICKEN DIJON

4 to 6 chicken breasts, boned
   and skinned
Finely crumbled seasoned
   bread crumbs

Dijon mustard

    Place chicken breasts in a greased baking dish and bake at 350°F. for 20 minutes. Remove from heat. Generously spread Dijon over chicken on both sides, then coat with bread crumbs and return to baking dish. Bake 45 minutes to 1 hour longer at 350°F. or until tender. The mustard gives the chicken a tangy flavor and makes it moist. Don't overcook. Serves 4 to 6.

DOROTHY TOWNSEND'S APRICOT CORNISH HENS

3 (1 lb.) Cornish hens,
   skinned
⅔ c. apricot nectar

3 Tbsp. apricot jam, melted

    Remove giblets from hens. Rinse hens under cold water and pat dry. Split each hen in half lengthwise, using an electric knife. Place hens in a 9x13 inch baking dish. Pour apricot nectar over them, turning to coat. Cover hens with fork and marinate in the refrigerator for 2 hours, turning occasionally. Remove hens from marinade, but reserve marinade.

    Bake, uncovered, in a 9x13 inch baking dish that is sprayed with a nonstick cooking spray at 350°F. for 20 minutes. Baste with marinade. Bake 20 minutes longer and baste with melted apricot jam. Bake 20 minutes more or until tender. Serves 6.

JANE BALLARD'S CAJUN CHICKEN

4 boneless, skinless chicken
   breast halves

Tabasco sauce
Onion powder

Rinse chicken in cool water and dry. Generously sprinkle Tabasco sauce on each side, then season each side with onion powder.

Spray skillet with a nonstick cooking spray. Place chicken in skillet and brown. Turn and brown other side. Cover and cook slowly until fork tender. Serves 4. Hot and spicy!

GRILLED CATALINA CHICKEN

4 skinless, boneless chicken
   breast halves

½ c. lowfat Catalina dressing
¼ tsp. black pepper

Trim all visible fat from chicken. Mix Catalina dressing and black pepper together. Pour into an oblong dish. Add chicken and turn to coat. Marinate chicken 4 to 6 hours or overnight.

When ready to grill, prepare coals and grill chicken for 20 minutes over hot grill. Brush chicken with reserved marinade. Serves 4.

ORANGE STUFFED ROAST TURKEY

1 (12 lb.) turkey, skinned
4 oranges, quartered
½ c. liquid Butter Buds (or
    nonfat butter-flavored
    cooking spray)

Wash and dry turkey. Remove giblets and neck.

Prepare Butter Buds as package directs to make ½ cup of liquid Butter Buds. Rub on outside of turkey. (Or, spray generously with a butter-flavored nonfat cooking spray.) Fill cavity with orange quarters.

Place turkey, breast up, on a rack in a roasting pan. Follow directions on turkey, wrapping for roasting, or roast at 325°F. for 3½ to 4 hours or until turkey is tender and juices run clear. Turkey should not be pink. Serves about 20.

HONEY HAM

1 boneless, fully-cooked   **½ c. packed brown sugar**
    ham
¼ c. honey

Score ham. Wrap in foil and bake for 1 hour at 325°F. in a broiler pan.

Combine and mix honey and brown sugar, blending well. Remove ham from oven. Pull foil open and spread honey glaze over ham. Rewrap in foil and bake for 1 hour longer. Cool for 15 minutes.

MARY ALICE LAWRENCE'S BAKED CHICKEN AND RICE CASSEROLE

4 to 6 chicken breasts
1 box Uncle Ben's long grain
  and wild rice (*not* instant)

1 (10¾ oz.) can cream of
  mushroom soup

In a greased 2½ quart size baking dish, mix 1 box rice and 2 cups hot water. Place chicken on top of rice. Bake, covered, at 375°F. for 1½ hours.

Dilute mushroom soup with water; mix it, then pour it over the chicken. Bake, uncovered, for 30 minutes, until soup bubbles and chicken is brown. Serves 4 to 6.

CHILI

2 lb. hamburger or ground
  round
2 pkg. Lawry's chili
  seasoning
2 (32 oz.) jars Ragu spaghetti
  sauce (with chunky
  tomatoes, onions, and
  peppers)

Brown meat in a heavy skillet; drain. Stir in seasoning mixes (dry). Add Ragu sauce and mix well. Simmer for 30 minutes. Serves 6.

Optional: Add 1 or 2 cans beans and heat for 20 minutes longer.

BARBECUED BEEF BRISKET

4 to 6 lb. brisket
1 (3½ oz.) bottle liquid
  smoke

6 to 8 oz. barbecue sauce

Place brisket in a baking pan. Pour liquid smoke over meat and rub it in. Cover and refrigerate overnight.

Next day, bake, covered, at 275°F. for 5 hours. Remove from oven. Slice. Pour barbecue sauce over brisket, then reheat before serving.

APRICOT GLAZED HAM

1 (29 oz.) can apricots
¾ c. apricot preserves

1 baked, boneless ham

Drain syrup from apricots. Reserve fruit. Bring syrup to a boil; reduce heat and simmer until amount is reduced to half, about 10 minutes. Remove from heat. Stir in preserves and apricots. Bake at 325°F. for 2 hours. Baste ham often with glaze during the last 30 minutes of baking and serve remainder along with ham.

ROSEBILLIE HORN'S OLD-FASHIONED ROAST BEEF

3 to 4 lb. beef roast
Seasoned flour

1 or 2 sliced onions

Dredge beef in seasoned flour. Place in greased skillet and brown on all sides to seal in juices. Lay sliced onions on top of roast. Pour ½ cup water over all. Cover and bake at 300°F. for 2½ hours. Remove cover and bake for 30 minutes longer.

Optional: After baking for 2 hours, add potatoes and carrots, then bake for 1 hour longer.

IRISH CHICKEN

1 chicken, cut into serving
** pieces**

1 slightly beaten egg
Dry potato flakes

Dip chicken piece in egg, then roll in Irish potato flakes. Repeat with all chicken pieces. Melt 1 stick margarine in a shallow baking pan, then place chicken in the pan and bake it for 30 minutes at 400°F. Turn chicken over and bake for 30 minutes more.

CHILI AND TAMALES

1 or 2 (15 oz.) cans tamales
1 or 2 (15 oz.) cans chili
   without beans

Shredded Cheddar cheese

Heat tamales and remove papers. Heat chili. Place 2 tamales on each serving plate. Pour hot chili over them and top with shredded cheese (or chopped onion).

BEVERLY BREJCHA'S TUNA BURGERS

1 (6⅛ oz.) can tuna fish,
   drained well
1 beaten egg

½ to 1 c. crushed Cheez-its
   crackers

Combine all ingredients and mix well. Shape into burgers. Brown on both sides in a skillet that has been sprayed with Pam nonstick cooking spray (or fry in a little vegetable oil). Serves 4.

BOB BATTERSON'S FRIED FISH FILLETS

8 fish fillets   1 tsp. Lawry's seasoning salt
1 c. Bisquick (or more)

Dip fish in Bisquick. Sprinkle with seasoning salt, then fry until golden brown on both sides. Allow 2 filets per person. Serves 4.

SOLE WITH YOGURT-DILL SAUCE

1 lb. sole fillets (3 oz. each)   ½ tsp. dill weed (or to taste)
1 c. lowfat plain yogurt

Saute fish in a nonstick skillet that has been sprayed with a nonfat cooking spray. Brown on both sides.

Mix yogurt with dill weed to taste. Pour over fish and heat. Serves 4.

Optional: Serve with lemon wedges.

PAT MEYERS' DILL PICKLE ROAST

1 (3 lb.) eye of round beef   Dill pickles
   roast
Juice from 1 pt. jar dill
   pickles

Place roast in a pan which has a lid. Pour juice over roast. Cover with lid or foil and bake at 325°F. for about 3 hours or until tender and done to your taste.

Serve pickles in a side dish with roast. Serves 12.

JUANITA'S STUFFED GREEN PEPPERS

1 lb. hamburger or ground   1 (16 oz.) can Spanish rice
   round, browned and   4 green peppers, seeded
   drained

Blanch green peppers in enough boiling water to cover; cool. Cut off tops of peppers; remove seeds and membranes. Stuff with mixture of cooked hamburger and Spanish rice. Bake at 350°F. for 20 minutes.

Optional: Stuff peppers that have not been boiled or blanched. Place them in a greased casserole and bake for 25 minutes at 350°F. Add a little water to the dish before baking the peppers.

CIDER HAM

1 cooked boneless ham
Whole cloves

2 c. apple cider

Score ham and place whole cloves in it. Pour a cup of cider over the ham. Cover and bake for 2 hours at 325°F. Baste occasionally with the second cup of cider.

HAMBURGER-POTATO CASSEROLE

2 lb. hamburger
1 (1 lb.) pkg. tater tots

1 (10¾ oz.) can cream of
mushroom soup

Form ingredients into 3 layers. Press hamburger as the bottom layer into a greased 9x12 inch pan. Spread soup over the meat. The tater tots form the third and top layer. Bake the casserole at 350°F. for 45 to 55 minutes. Drain off any excess grease from the hamburger.

Optional: Potatoes could be second layer, then top with soup.

TERRI BAHR'S GOULASH

1 lb. hamburger or ground
    round
½ pkg. shell macaroni
1 (16 oz.) jar Ragu spaghetti
    sauce (with chunky
    tomatoes and onions)

    Prepare macaroni as package directs. Brown meat and drain. Combine and mix the ingredients together. Simmer until hot.

PORK CHOP SPECIAL

1 c. rice, cooked
4 to 6 pork chops

2 (10¾ oz.) cans cream of
    mushroom soup

    Brown pork chops on both sides; drain. Place cooked rice in bottom of a greased baking dish. Lay browned chops over rice. Pour soup over pork chops. Bake for 30 to 45 minutes at 375°F.

CHICKEN MOZZARELLA

6 chicken breasts, halved,
    skinned, and boned
1 (12 oz.) jar Prego spaghetti
    sauce

6 slices Mozzarella cheese

Place chicken breasts in a greased baking dish. Cover with sauce. Bake, covered, for 1 hour at 325°F. Remove from oven. Top each breast with 1 slice cheese. Return to oven and bake, uncovered, for 10 minutes longer.

Serve with spaghetti or noodles, if desired.

TUNA-CHIP CASSEROLE

1 (6 oz.) can tuna fish,
    drained
2 c. crushed potato chips

1 or 2 (10¾ oz.) cans cream
    of mushroom soup

Place a layer of crushed potato chips in a greased casserole dish. Top with a layer of tuna. Repeat layers. Pour mushroom soup over tuna and bake for 25 minutes at 350°F. Serves 2 to 4.

EGGS IN A NEST

4 slices bread   **2 Tbsp. margarine**
4 eggs

Use a 2 inch cookie cutter to cut circles in center of each slice of bread. Remove bread circles and save for another use. Spread margarine on bread and fry it on one side. Add more margarine if needed. Turn bread over. Break egg into a cup and gently pour egg into center of bread. Place cover on skillet and cook for 3 to 5 minutes, until egg is as firm as desired. Serves 4.

HAM AND NOODLES ROMANOFF

1 box noodles Romanoff mix   **1 (8 oz.) can cut green beans,**
1½ c. cooked ham, cubed   **drained**

Prepare noodles according to package directions, but increase milk to ⅔ cup. Stir in ham and green beans. Bake in a greased 1½ quart casserole dish, covered, for 20 minutes at 350°F. Serves 4.

HAWAIIAN HAM STEAKS

Center cut ham steak (¾ inch
   thick)
2 Tbsp. brown sugar

1 (8½ oz.) can sliced
   pineapple (with juice)

    Pour ½ inch juice into a skillet. Stir in 2 tablespoons brown sugar. Make slashes in fat around steak to keep it from curling. Place ham in skillet with juice. Top with pineapple slices. Cook on medium low heat. Turn twice. Cook until sauce becomes a thick syrup. Serve with pineapple slice on each serving. Serves 4.

OLIVE-EGG SALAD SANDWICH SPREAD

1 (8 oz.) jar green stuffed
   olives, drained

6 boiled eggs
Mayonnaise

    Slice olives. Hard-boil eggs. Rinse eggs in cool water. Peel off shells and chop eggs. Combine eggs, olives, and enough mayonnaise to moisten. Refrigerate until ready to use. Spread on wheat toast and cut in half for sandwiches. Serves 4 to 6.

WILLIE COPELAND'S
SOUTHERN FRIED CHICKEN

1 (2 to 2½ lb.) fryer chicken,   1½ to 2 c. flour
    cut in serving pieces   1 to 1½ inches oil

    Put flour (and desired seasonings) in a brown paper bag and shake 2 or 3 pieces of chicken at a time in it until chicken is well-coated. Remove chicken from bag and shake off excess. Heat oil in a deep skillet (at least 1 to 1½ inches of oil). Place chicken, skin side down, in hot oil. Cook, covered, for 5 minutes. Remove cover and fry until bottom side is browned. Turn chicken once and fry on other side. Drain on paper towels. Serves 4.

    Total cooking time is 30 to 40 minutes.

SWISS STEAK

2 lb. round steak   1 (16 oz.) can tomato sauce
1 sliced onion   with onions and
                    peppers

    Trim fat and pound steak. Place in a greased 9x13 inch pan. Top with onion slices, then pour tomato sauce over it. Cover and bake at 350°F. for 1½ hours. Uncover and bake for 15 minutes longer. Baste occasionally with tomato sauce. Bake until tender. Serves 4 to 6.

MARILYN WEAVER'S SAUCE FOR BRISKET

1 (8 to 10 oz.) bottle Heinz   1 (12 oz.) can Coca-Cola
   chili sauce   1 pkg. onion soup mix

Combine the 3 ingredients and mix well. Makes 2½ cups of sauce.

To prepare: Place brisket in roaster with a lid. Pour sauce over it. Cover and bake at 325°F. for 3 to 5 hours, or for 30 minutes per pound, or until tender. Pour off sauce and serve in a gravy bowl with brisket.

ONITA COPELAND'S CHICKEN FRIED STEAK

1 lb. Minute steaks or sirloin   1 or 2 beaten eggs
   steak, cut in serving   Flour
   pieces

Roll steaks in flour and dip in well beaten egg, then roll in flour again. Fry in hot oil (or Pam cooking spray) until browned. Serves 2 to 3.

CHICKEN JALAPENO

4 skinned and boned chicken   ½ c. jalapeno jelly
   breast halves
2 Tbsp. melted butter or
   margarine

    Place chicken breasts between 2 sheets of heavy-duty plastic wrap and flatten to ¼ inch thickness, using a meat mallet.

    Cook chicken in butter in a large skillet over medium heat for 5 minutes on each side. Remove to a serving platter. Stir jelly into pan drippings and bring to a boil, stirring until smooth. Spoon over chicken. Serves 4.

AMISH PORK ROAST

1 (3 to 4 lb.) pork roast   3 c. water
1 (27 oz.) can sauerkraut

    Place pork roast in center of roast pan. Arrange sauerkraut around meat. Pour water over roast. Cover and bake at 325°F. for 2½ to 3 hours. Serves 8 to 12.

    Add more water if sauerkraut dries during baking.

SAUSAGE DRESSING

1 box Pepperidge Farm herb
   stuffing mix

1 lb. bulk sausage (R.B. Rice)
1 c. chopped onion

Prepare stuffing according to package directions. Brown and drain sausage. Remove sausage from skillet and saute onions in the drippings. Combine dressing, sausage, and onions; mix well. Pour into a greased casserole dish and bake for 30 minutes at 325°F. Serves 6 to 8.

Serve with turkey or chicken.

CROCK POT ROAST BEEF

1 (3 to 4 lb.) roast
2 onions, sliced

4 potatoes, peeled and
   quartered

Place half of the potatoes and onions in the bottom of a crock pot. Lay beef roast on top of the vegetables, then add the remaining potatoes and onions on top of the meat. Pour ½ cup water over the meat and vegetables. Cover and cook on LOW for 10 to 12 hours or on HIGH for 5 to 6 hours.

CHIPPED BEEF IN PATTY SHELLS

1 pkg. frozen patty shells   Parsley
1 or 2 pkg. frozen Stouffer's
    creamed chipped beef

     Bake patty shells according to package directions. Prepare chipped beef as package directs. To serve, place a patty shell in each serving plate and fill with chipped beef. Top with a sprig of parsley.

PACKAGED STEAK DINNER

4 sirloin tip steaks   4 sliced potatoes
1 to 2 sliced onions

     Place meat on foil and top with layers of sliced onions and potatoes. Seal foil into packages and place them in a pan. Bake for 1 hour at 350°F.

CREAM CHEESE, WALNUTS, AND OLIVE SANDWICH SPREAD

1 (8 oz.) pkg. cream cheese,
   softened
¼ c. chopped black walnuts

½ c. stuffed green olives,
   sliced or chopped

Combine, mix well, and spread on whole wheat toast.

SAUSAGE AND APPLES

1 lb. sausage
Jonathan apples, sliced

Brown sugar

Shape sausage into patties and fry or broil until well done; drain. Sprinkle brown sugar over apples and cook slowly in a saucepan. Add dots of butter if desired. Serve sausage over apples.

ROAST CHICKEN

1 whole chicken   5 Tbsp. melted margarine
1 onion, peeled

    Rinse chicken inside and out with cool water. Dry with paper towels. Place a peeled onion inside chicken cavity. Brush margarine over chicken. Tie legs together. Place in a foil lined broiler pan and roast chicken at 350°F. for 20 minutes per pound. Baste often with additional margarine. Chicken is done when it is pricked with a fork and the juice is clear.

CRESCENT PIZZA

1 (8 oz.) can crescent dinner   1 (6 oz.) pkg. shredded
  rolls   Mozzarella cheese
1 (3½ oz.) pkg. pepperoni
  slices

    Separate crescent rolls into 4 rectangles and seal perforations. Arrange 8 pepperoni slices on each 5x7 inch rectangle. Top with cheese. Place on a greased baking sheet and bake for 14 to 16 minutes at 375°F., or until crust is golden brown.

    Optional: Before placing pepperoni and cheese on pizza, spread a prepared spaghetti sauce such as Ragu or Prego on the crescent roll dough, then top it with pepperoni and cheese and bake.

BROILED T-BONE STEAKS

4 T-bone steaks　　　　**1 tsp. garlic powder (or to**
2 Tbsp. margarine　　　　　**taste)**

Make a few diagonal cuts in the fat around the steak so it won't curl when broiling. Place the steaks on the broiler pan, which has been lined with foil.

Broil 5 minutes on one side. Turn and broil 5 minutes on the other side. Continue cooking to desired doneness if steaks are too rare.

Mix margarine and garlic. Put a dollop on each steak. Serves 4.

ANN'S BEEF FONDUE

Filet mignon, cut into 1 inch　　**2 c. vegetable oil**
**　cubes**　　　　　　　　　　**Sauce of your choice**

Prepare ½ pound filet per person. Heat 2 cups oil on stove until hot. *Watch carefully.* Pour oil into fondue pot. Place pot on table above burner. Give each person his own fondue fork. Spear meat on fork and cook in oil in fondue pot to desired doneness. Remove meat to plate and dip in choice of spices offered (such as mustard sauce, sour cream and onion sauce, chili sauce, B.B.Q. sauce, etc.).

BEEF TIPS AND NOODLES

1½ lb. stew meat (boneless),   1 (8 oz.) pkg. noodles
 trimmed
2 (10½ oz.) cans cream of
 onion soup, diluted

Brown stew meat in a greased skillet. When browned, add soup which has been partially diluted. Allow to simmer for 3 hours, stirring occasionally.

Cook noodles according to package directions. Serve beef tips over noodles.

Note: When diluting soup, use only 1 can water.

JOHN BEUSCHER'S INCREDIBLE RIBS

Slab of ribs   Italian dressing
Lawry's seasoning

Spread coals evenly in grill. Open bottom vent ½ way and light coals. Place ribs, bone down, in bottom layer of foil. "Paint" ribs with dressing. Sprinkle with seasoning. Cover top with foil. When fire is out on coals, place wrapped ribs on grill and cover. Close top vent till only a slit is visible. Cook for 6 hours, turning ribs every 2 hours. At hour 6, remove foil top and puncture bottom foil to drain.

Optional: Coat with BBQ sauce and cook 45 to 60 minutes more.

CARAWAY SEED ROAST

1 (3 lb.) rump roast (or your
    choice of roast)

Caraway seed
Salt (plain or garlic salt)

Trim all visible fat from meat. Sprinkle caraway seeds and salt over a rump roast. Place on rack in roaster and cover or wrap in foil and bake dry at 325°F. for 3 hours or until tender.

The caraway seeds give a good flavor. The drippings make a delicious gravy. (But remember, gravy is high in cholesterol.) Serves 8 to 12.

BETTY JO'S MUSHROOM CHICKEN

4 chicken breast halves,
    skinned and boned
1 (10¾ oz.) can cream of
    mushroom soup

1 c. sour cream

Combine mushroom soup and sour cream and pour over chicken breasts (which have been placed in a greased 9x13 inch pan).

Bake 3 hours at 250°F. or until fork tender. If you're in a hurry, you could bake it 1 hour at 350°F. Don't overcook. Serves 4.

PARTY BRISKET

1 (5 lb.) beef brisket
1 (6 oz.) can frozen lemon
  juice concentrate

1 env. Lipton dry onion soup
  mix

Trim off all visible fat from meat. Stir enough thawed lemon juice concentrate into the onion soup mix to make a smooth paste.

Place brisket in a 9x13 inch pan or in a roasting pan. Spread lemon-onion paste over meat. Cover tightly with foil or a lid. Bake at 250°F. for 5 to 6 hours or until fork tender. Serves 10 to 12.

Optional: Stir a little Worcestershire sauce into lemon-onion paste; spread on brisket, then bake.

TEXAS BRISKET

1 (6 lb.) boneless beef brisket
2 Tbsp. Worcestershire
  sauce

1 small bottle liquid smoke

Place brisket in a covered pan. Pour sauce and smoke over it. Cover and bake at 250°F. for 5 to 7 hours or until tender. Serves 18 to 20.

HAM JUBILEE

1 (1½ lb.) fully cooked
   smoked ham slice (1
   inch thick)

¼ tsp. cloves
1 (21 oz.) can cherry pie
   filling

Place 1 fully cooked smoked ham slice in a greased 9x13 inch pan. Sprinkle with cloves. Cover and bake at 350°F. for 30 minutes, or until heated throughout. Cut into serving pieces. Pour ½ can cherry pie filling into a saucepan and heat, stirring often. Serve as an accompaniment to ham in a separate bowl. Spoon over ham. Serves 4.

BROILED CHICKEN CORDON BLEU

4 chicken breast halves,
   skinned and boned
4 slices Cheddar or Swiss
   cheese

4 slices ham or Canadian
   bacon (fully cooked)

Preheat broiler. Broil chicken breasts 4 inches from heat for 4 minutes. Turn chicken over and broil for 4 or 5 minutes, or until tender. Cut cheese in halves. Place ½ slice cheese on top of each chicken breast, then top the cheese with a thin ham or Canadian bacon slice. Broil for about ½ minute, then top with remaining ½ cheese slices. Broil until cheese melts. Serves 4.

CORNED BEEF AND CABBAGE

4 to 6 lb. corned beef   6 potatoes
   boneless brisket
1 head cabbage, cored and
   quartered

Cover beef with cold water and bring to a boil. Lower heat and simmer for 4 hours, or until tender. Add potatoes and cook for 20 minutes. Add cabbage and cook for about 12 minutes longer, or until all 3 ingredients are fork tender. Serves 8 to 12.

Optional: Add onion, cut in quarters.

HAMBURGER STEAK WITH MUSHROOMS

1½ lb. hamburger or ground   ½ lb. mushrooms, sliced
   round steak   3 to 4 Tbsp. margarine

Shape hamburger or ground round steak into 4 large patties. Fry on both sides to desired doneness. In a separate skillet, melt margarine. Saute clean, sliced mushrooms in melted margarine, stirring often, for about 5 minutes. Drain. Place a hamburger steak on each dinner plate. Top with sauteed mushrooms. Serves 4.

DESIREE WORNALL'S
BAKED MACARONI AND CHEESE

2 c. macaroni (8 oz. pkg.)   1 (8 oz.) ctn. Velveeta
2⅓ c. milk   cheese, cubed

    Cook macaroni as package directs until tender. Drain. Stir in milk and cheese. Mix well. Pour into a greased baking dish and bake at 350°F. for about 1 to 1¼ hours or until set and browned. Serves 6.

ROAST LOIN OF PORK

1 (3 oz.) boneless pork loin   1 tsp. marjoram leaves
    roast
1 tsp. powdered mustard

    Place roast on a rack in a shallow baking pan. Combine dry mustard and marjoram leaves; rub over surface of roast. Insert a meat thermometer, if desired, and roast at 350°F. for *30 to 35 minutes per pound* or until the thermometer reads 170°F. and meat is done. Pork should be cooked thoroughly. Slice and serve. Serves 8 to 12.

    Baking time: 1½ to 2 hours.

PENNSYLVANIA DUTCH PORK AND SAUERKRAUT

1 (2 to 2½ lb.) tenderloin of
    pork
2 Tbsp. margarine
1 (2 lb.) pkg. sauerkraut with
    juice (or 2 (16 oz.) cans
    sauerkraut)

Melt margarine in a heavy iron skillet or Dutch oven and brown the pork on both sides. Cover and cook tenderloin over low heat for 20 minutes. Add sauerkraut. Cover and continue to simmer for 1 hour, or until tenderloin is thoroughly cooked. (Pork should never be pink.)

Serve with mashed potatoes and applesauce for an authentic Pennsylvania Dutch dinner. Serves 4 to 6.

BAKED LEMONADE CHICKEN

6 chicken breasts, split,
    boned, and skinned (or
    use any chicken pieces
    desired)

1 (6 oz.) can frozen lemonade
    concentrate, thawed
⅓ c. margarine

Pour thawed lemonade concentrate into a 9x13 inch Pyrex dish; cover and marinate chicken in it for 1 hour in refrigerator, turning often to coat well.

Melt margarine in a pan. Drain chicken, then place in prepared, buttered pan and bake at 350°F. for about 1 hour or until tender. Serves 6.

Optional: Pour marinade over chicken before baking.

BAKED BUTTERMILK CHICKEN

1 chicken, cut in serving
    pieces
½ c. buttermilk

1 c. Vigo Italian style bread
    crumbs

Dip chicken in buttermilk, then roll it in bread crumbs. Place on a nonstick baking pan, sprayed with Pam cooking spray. Bake at 350°F. for 45 minutes or until tender. Serves 4.

Note: Vigo bread crumbs comes in an 8 ounce can and is usually in the bread section at the supermarket.

PEPPERONI CHICKEN

6 chicken breasts, halved,
    skinned, and boned

1 pkg. pepperoni slices
Mozzarella cheese slices

Brown chicken on both sides in a well-greased skillet. Place chicken in a greased pan. Arrange 4 pepperoni slices over each and bake 10 to 15 minutes. Remove from oven, top each with cheese, and bake 5 to 10 minutes or until chicken is tender. Serves 6.

LEG OF LAMB

1 (6 lb.) leg of lamb   **2 c. Heinz cider vinegar**
2 c. water

Combine and mix water and vinegar. Pour into a roaster. Rub mixture over lamb. Place lamb on roaster rack. Cover and cook at 400°F. for 3 hours *(30 minutes per pound)*. Baste frequently. Remove cover to let lamb brown and cook 15 minutes longer. Good with mint sauce.

CREAMED DRIED BEEF

¼ lb. thinly sliced dried beef,   **3 Tbsp. flour**
   chipped   **2 to 3 c. hot milk**

Fry thin dried beef slices in a well greased skillet until crisp. Stir in flour with the beef, then slowly add the milk and cook until thickened, stirring constantly. (The beef is so salty that no salt should be added.) Serve hot over crisp toast.

Note: Dried beef is very salty. You might want to rinse off some salt before preparing this recipe.

Notes

Breads, Rolls

MICROWAVE HINTS

1. Place an open box of hardened brown sugar in the microwave oven with 1 cup hot water. Microwave at high for 1½ to 2 minutes for ½ pound or 2 to 3 minutes for 1 pound.
2. Soften hard ice cream by microwaving at 30% power. One pint will take 15 to 30 seconds; one quart, 30 to 45 seconds; and one-half gallon, 45 seconds to one minute.
3. One stick of butter or margarine will soften in 1 minute when microwaved at 20% power.
4. Soften one 8-ounce package of cream cheese by microwaving at 30% power for 2 to 2½ minutes. One 3-ounce package of cream cheese will soften in 1½ to 2 minutes.
5. Thaw frozen orange juice right in the container. Remove the top metal lid. Place the opened container in the microwave and heat on high power 30 seconds for 6 ounces and 45 seconds for 12 ounces.
6. Thaw whipped topping...a 4½ ounce carton will thaw in 1 minute on the defrost setting. Whipped topping should be slightly firm in the center but it will blend well when stirred. Do not overthaw!
7. Soften jello that has set up too hard - perhaps you were to chill it until slightly thickened and forgot it. Heat on a low power setting for a very short time.
8. Dissolve gelatin in the microwave. Measure liquid in a measuring cup, add jello and heat. There will be less stirring to dissolve the gelatin.
9. Heat hot packs in a microwave oven. A wet fingertip towel will take about 25 seconds. It depends on the temperature of the water used to wet the towel.
10. To scald milk, cook 1 cup milk for 2-2½ minutes, stirring once each minute.
11. To make dry bread crumbs, cut 6 slices bread into ½-inch cubes. Microwave in 3-quart casserole 6-7 minutes, or until dry, stirring after 3 minutes. Crush in blender.
12. Refresh stale potato chips, crackers, or other snacks of such type by putting a plateful in the microwave oven for about 30-45 seconds. Let stand for 1 minute to crisp. Cereals can also be crisped.
13. Melt almond bark for candy or dipping pretzels. One pound will take about 2 minutes, stirring twice. If it hardens while dipping candy, microwave for a few seconds longer.
14. Nuts will be easier to shell if you place 2 cups of nuts in a 1-quart casserole with 1 cup of water. Cook for 4 to 5 minutes and the nut meats will slip out whole after cracking the shell.
15. When thawing hamburger meat, the outside will many times begin cooking before the meat is completely thawed. Defrost for 3 minutes, then remove the outside portions that have defrosted. Continue defrosting the hamburger, taking off the defrosted outside portions at short intervals.
16. To drain the fat from hamburger while it is cooking in the microwave oven (one pound cooks in 5 minutes on high), cook it in a plastic colander placed inside a casserole dish.
17. Cubed meat and chopped vegetables will cook more evenly if cut uniformly.
18. When baking large cakes, brownies, or moist bars, place a juice glass in the center of the baking dish to prevent a soggy middle and ensure uniform baking throughout.
19. Since cakes and quick breads rise higher in a microwave oven, fill pans just half full of batter.
20. For stamp collectors: Place a few drops of water on stamp to be removed from envelope. Heat in the microwave for 20 seconds and the stamp will come right off.
21. Using a round dish instead of a square one eliminates overcooked corners in baking cakes.
22. When preparing chicken in a dish, place meaty pieces around the edges and the bony pieces in the center of the dish.
23. Shaping meatloaf into a ring eliminates undercooked center. A glass set in the center of a dish can serve as the mold.
24. Treat fresh meat cuts for 15 to 20 seconds on high in the microwave oven. This cuts down on meat-spoiling types of bacteria.
25. A crusty coating of chopped walnuts surrounding many microwave-cooked cakes and quick breads enhances the looks and eating quality. Sprinkle a layer of medium finely chopped walnuts evenly onto the bottom and sides of a ring pan or Bundt cake pan. Pour in batter and microwave as recipe directs.
26. Do not salt foods on the surface as it causes dehydration (meats and vegetables) and toughens the food. Salt the meat after you remove it from the oven unless the recipe calls for using salt in the mixture.
27. Heat leftover custard and use it as frosting for a cake.
28. Melt marshmallow creme in the microwave oven. Half of a 7-ounce jar will melt in 35-40 seconds on high. Stir to blend.
29. Toast coconut in the microwave. Watch closely because it browns quickly once it begins to brown. Spread ½ cup coconut in a pie plate and cook for 3-4 minutes, stirring every 30 seconds after 2 minutes.
30. Place a cake dish up on another dish or on a roasting rack if you have difficulty getting the bottom of the cake done. This also works for potatoes and other foods that don't quite get done on the bottom.

BREADS, ROLLS

PARTY BISCUITS

1 c. self-rising flour
1 c. whipping cream (not
   whipped)

2 Tbsp. sugar

   Mix together and pour into greased mini-muffin cups. Bake 10 minutes at 400°F. Yield: 1½ to 2 dozen.

LUCY HETZEL'S MOZZARELLA CHEESE LOAF

1 small loaf unsliced French
   or Italian bread

Sliced Mozzarella cheese
Softened margarine

   Slice bread almost all the way through at ½ inch intervals. Place Mozzarella slices between the slices of bread and brush the loaf generously with margarine. Place on a greased baking sheet and bake at 450°F. for 10 minutes, or until cheese melts and bread is golden brown. Serves 6.

BUTTERMILK BISCUITS

½ c. margarine
2 c. self-rising flour

¾ c. buttermilk

Cut ½ cup margarine into flour with a pastry blender until mixture resembles coarse meal. Stir in buttermilk and mix until dry ingredients are moistened. Turn dough out onto a floured surface and knead 3 or 4 times.

Roll dough to ¾ inch thickness, then cut with a biscuit cutter. Place on a lightly greased cookie sheet and bake at 425°F. for 12 to 15 minutes. Brush with additional melted margarine, if desired. Serves 6.

ICE CREAM MUFFINS

2 c. self-rising flour
1 pt. vanilla ice cream

Margarine or butter

Blend together flour and ice cream until well moistened. The batter will be lumpy. Fill 10 well-buttered muffin cups ¾ full and bake at 350°F. for 20 minutes. Serves 5 to 10.

MEXICAN CORN BREAD

1 (8½ oz.) pkg. Jiffy corn bread mix

1 small can cream-style corn
½ c. shredded Cheddar cheese

Prepare corn bread according to package directions. Stir in corn and ¼ cup shredded cheese. Pour into a greased skillet or muffin tins. Top with remaining ¼ cup cheese. Bake at 400°F. for 15 to 20 minutes. Serves 4.

MAYONNAISE ROLLS

2 c. self-rising flour
1 c. milk

4 Tbsp. mayonnaise

Combine, mix, and pour into greased muffin tins. Bake at 400°F. for 22 minutes. Serves 6 to 8.

HOT CHEESY SLICES

½ lb. grated Cheddar cheese
1 c. mayonnaise
4 to 6 sourdough French
   rolls, cut in ½ inch
   slices (or French bread
   could be used)

Mix together cheese and mayonnaise. Spread on bread slices. Place bread on cookie sheet and bake 8 to 10 minutes at 350°F.

For variety, sometimes I mix 2 cheeses, Cheddar and Swiss, with mayonnaise and spread on the bread. Serves 4 to 6.

JILL RUIZ'S COFFEE CAKE

1 loaf frozen bread, thawed   Sugar-cinnamon mixture
½ pt. whipping cream

Spread dough into a greased 9x13 inch pan. Let rise. Poke several times with finger. Sprinkle sugar mixture over it. Pour cream evenly over top. Bake 20 minutes at 350°F. or until golden brown.

CHEESE PUFFS

1 can biscuits   Vegetable oil
12 cubes Cheddar cheese

Separate biscuits and roll out or press out flat. Place a cheese cube in the center. Shape into a ball. Drop in boiling oil. Deep-fry until golden and puffy. Drain on paper towels.

ROSEBILLIE HORN'S ZUCCHINI BREAD

1 box spice cake mix   ½ c. chopped black walnuts
2 c. shredded zucchini   or pecans

Prepare cake mix as box directs. Squeeze liquid out of zucchini, then stir it and the nuts into the spice cake. Mix well. Pour into 2 greased and floured loaf pans. Bake at 350°F. for 50 to 60 minutes.

NO-PEEK POPOVERS

2 eggs   1 c. flour
1 c. milk

Combine and mix well. Pour into 8 greased muffin cups ¾ full. Place in a *cold* 450°F. oven. Bake for 30 minutes and don't peek! Yield: 8 popovers.

CHEESE STICKS

1 loaf French bread   1 stick margarine
   (unsliced)
1 glass Old English cheese

Combine cheese and margarine; beat until smooth and soft enough to spread. Slice bread 1 inch thick. Remove crusts. Cut each into 3 sticks. Spread 3 sides and ends with cheese mixture. Bake for 10 minutes at 350°F.

Hint: Cube the bread crusts that were removed and toss them with margarine and garlic salt. Bake until brown to use as croutons.

CAROLE'S EASY DRESSING

1 (6 oz.) box Stove Top corn
    bread stuffing mix
1 chopped onion

1 (10½ oz.) can chicken broth
    (skim off fat)

Combine stuffing mix, the contents of the vegetable seasoning packet (that comes with the stuffing), the chopped onion, and the broth in a mixing bowl and mix well.

Spray a baking dish with a nonstick cooking spray. Pour dressing into prepared dish and bake at 325°F. for 30 minutes.

Each ½ cup serving contains 150 calories and 3 fat grams.

Optional: Add chopped celery to dressing before baking.

CLOVERLEAF ROLLS

2¼ c. reduced fat biscuit mix,
    divided

1 (8 oz.) ctn. sour cream
    (lowfat)
½ c. melted margarine
    (lowfat)

Combine 2 cups biscuit mix with sour cream and melted butter and mix well. Sprinkle the remaining ¼ cup of biscuit mix on sheet of waxed paper. Drop dough by level tablespoonfuls onto biscuit mix and roll into balls. Place 3 balls into each of 12 greased muffin cups. Bake at 350°F. for 15 to 20 minutes or until golden brown. Yield: 1 dozen.

Contains 150 calories per roll.

SOUR CREAM ROLLS

1 c. sour cream   1 c. self-rising flour
½ c. melted margarine

    Combine flour, oleo, and sour cream; mix. Pour into greased *miniature muffin tins* and bake at 450°F. for 15 minutes. Yield: 12 rolls.

MINI SWEET ROLLS

Margarine   1 pkg. Pillsbury crescent rolls
Brown sugar

    In greased *miniature muffin pans,* place ½ teaspoon margarine and ½ teaspoon brown sugar in each cup.

    Take 1 package Pillsbury crescent rolls and roll out. Take 2 squares; press together the creases. Roll up tightly. Slice each roll in 6 slices. Lay a slice in each muffin cup on top of oleo and brown sugar. Bake at 375°F. for 10 to 12 minutes. Yield: 12 rolls.

Desserts

Common Baking Dishes and Pans

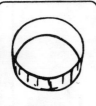
Spring Form Pan

Layer Cake or Pie Pan

Ring Mold

Baking or Square Pan

Loaf Pan

Brioche Pan

Angel Cake Pan

Bundt Tube

Equivalent Dishes

4-CUP BAKING DISH
= 9" pie plate
= 8" x $1^1 4$" layer cake pan
= $7^3 8$" x $3^5 8$" x $2^1 4$" loaf pan

6-CUP BAKING DISH
= 8" or 9" x $1^1 2$" layer cake pan
= 10" pie pan
= $8^1 2$" x $3^5 8$" x $2^5 8$" loaf pan

8-CUP BAKING DISH
= 8" x 8" x 2" square pan
= 11" x 7" x $1^1 2$" baking pan
= 9" x 5" x 3" loaf pan

10-CUP BAKING DISH
= 9" x 9" x 2" square pan
= $11^3 4$" x $7^1 2$" x $1^3 4$" baking pan
= 15" x 10" x 1" flat jelly roll pan

12-CUP BAKING DISH OR MORE
= $13^1 2$" x $8^1 2$" x 2" glass baking dish
= 13" x 9" x 2" metal baking pan
= 14" x $10^1 2$" x $2^1 2$" roasting pan

Total Volume of Pans

TUBE PANS

$7^1 2$" x 3" Bundt tube	6 cups
9" x $3^1 2$" fancy or Bundt tube	9 cups
9" x $3^1 2$" angel cake pan	12 cups
10" x $3^3 4$" Bundt tube	12 cups
9" x $3^1 2$" fancy tube mold	12 cups
10" x 4" fancy tube mold	16 cups
10" x 4" angel cake pan	18 cups

SPRING FORM PANS

8" x 3" pan	12 cups
9" x 3" pan	16 cups

RING MOLDS

$8^1 2$" x $2^1 4$" mold	$4^1 2$ cups
$9^1 4$" x $2^3 4$" mold	8 cups

BRIOCHE PAN

$9^1 2$" x $3^1 4$" pan	8 cups

DESSERTS

❖   ❖   ❖

SPEEDY BANANA PIE

2 to 3 sliced bananas
1 baked, cooled pie crust

1 (4 oz.) box prepared
   banana pudding

Place banana slices in cooled crust. Pour pudding over bananas. Garnish with banana slices. Let stand 5 to 10 minutes. Serves 6.

Optional: For a speedy meringue, sprinkle 2 cups miniature marshmallows over top of pie and broil 2 to 3 minutes until light brown and partially melted.

CHOCOLATE ALMOND PIE

1 (8 oz.) *Hershey's* chocolate
   almond bar
1 small tub Cool Whip

1 (8 inch) graham cracker
   prepared crust

Melt Hershey's bar in top of a double boiler. Remove from heat and cool. Stir Cool Whip into chocolate. Fill the pie crust and chill.

Garnish, if desired, by using a potato peeler to shave chocolate curls off a Hershey's candy bar. Serves 6 to 8.

FROZEN LEMONADE PIE

1 small can frozen pink
   lemonade (or limeade)
1 small ctn. Cool Whip

1 (14 oz.) can Eagle Brand
   condensed,
   sweetened milk

Combine lemonade, Cool Whip, and Eagle Brand milk. Mix well; chill. Serve as pudding or pour into a pie crust (graham cracker) and freeze. Serves 6 to 8.

CHERRY COBBLER

1 (21 oz.) can Wilderness
   cherry pie filling
1 to 2 sticks margarine,
   sliced

1 box yellow or white cake
   mix (dry)

Spread cherry pie filling in a greased 9x13 inch baking dish. Sprinkle with cake mix. Top with slices of margarine. Bake at 350°F. for about 35 minutes. Delicious served with a dip of vanilla ice cream. Serves 8.

Note: Any pie filling or canned fruit could be substituted for the cherries.

STRAWBERRY ICE CREAM PIE

1 (3 oz.) pkg. strawberry Jell-
   O
1 pt. vanilla ice cream

1 pt. fresh or frozen
   strawberries

Prepare Jell-O with 1 cup boiling water. Mix well until Jell-O is dissolved. Stir in the ice cream, then the berries. Chill and serve as pudding or pour into a prepared pie crust. Serves 6.

SHAKER LEMON PIE

2 lemons, sliced thin (rind
   and all)

1½ c. sugar
4 eggs

Place lemon slices in a bowl; pour sugar over them. Mix well and let stand 2 to 3 hours.

Beat 4 eggs and pour over lemons. Fill an uncooked pie crust. Add a top crust. Make vents in top crust. Bake at 450°F. for 15 minutes. Reduce heat to 350°F. and bake until done. Serves 8.

GRANNY'S PEACH COBBLER

1 (29 oz.) can sliced peaches   ½ c. melted margarine
   (with syrup)
1 (18¼ oz.) pkg. butter pecan
   cake mix or 1 yellow
   cake mix

Spread peaches in a greased 9x13 inch pan. Sprinkle dry cake mix over all. Drizzle margarine over cake mix. Bake at 325°F. for 45 to 55 minutes. Serves 8.

Note: This recipe was given to me by my 99 year old Granny, Anna Davis of Harrison, Arkansas, who lives alone and takes care of a 4 bedroom home, cooks, makes a garden, writes songs, quilts, crochets, sews, and has written and published 2 books of poetry.

BLUEBERRY PIE A LA MODE

1 (21 oz.) can blueberry pie   Vanilla ice cream
   filling
1 (8 inch) double pie crust (or
   graham cracker crust

Line pie pan with rolled pie crust. Spread blueberry filling evenly in crust. Place top crust over filling and press edges together. Cut vents in it. Bake at 425°F. for 10 minutes. Reduce heat to 350°F. and bake for 25 to 35 minutes longer, or until the crust is golden brown. Cool. Slice. Place slice on dessert plate and top with dip of ice cream. Serves 6 to 8.

Optional: Pour blueberries into a prepared graham cracker crust and top with ice cream.

FROZEN STRAWBERRY YOGURT PIE

16 oz. strawberry yogurt   **9 inch graham cracker crust**
8 oz. Cool Whip   **or an Oreo chocolate**
                                                          crust

   Combine and mix yogurt and whipped cream. Pour into crust and freeze. Garnish with fresh strawberries, if desired. Serves 6 to 8.

STRAWBERRY PIE FILLING

2 pt. strawberries   **1 c. sugar**
3 Tbsp. cornstarch

   Mash 1 pint strawberries. Combine cornstarch and sugar in a saucepan. Gradually add mashed berries, stirring constantly until thickened. Cool.

   Optional: Pour remaining berries in baked pie crust. Cover with strawberry mixture. Refrigerate until set.

CHOCOLATE PUDDING OR PIE FILLING

1 (14 oz.) can Eagle Brand
   sweetened condensed
   milk

3 sq. semi-sweet chocolate
½ c. boiling water

Heat Eagle Brand milk. Blend in chocolate and stir until melted. Mix in ½ cup boiling water. Stir constantly until mixture thickens, about 5 minutes. Serve chilled in dessert dishes.

Optional: Pour into a baked pie crust and top with meringue.

COCONUT CREAM PIE

1 (3 oz.) pkg. vanilla pie
   filling mix

1 (6 oz.) pkg. coconut
1 baked pie shell

Prepare pudding as package directs; cool. Stir in coconut. Mix well and pour into a baked pie crust. Refrigerate for 4 hours before serving.

Optional: Top with meringue or Cool Whip.

BRICKLE CHIP ICE CREAM PIE

½ gal. vanilla ice cream
1 c. brickle chips
1 (9 inch) graham cracker
   crumb pie crust or
   chocolate pie crust

Spoon half of vanilla ice cream into pie crust. Spread ⅔ cup brickle chips over. Heap with remaining ice cream and sprinkle top with ½ cup brickle chips. Freeze.

If desired, serve with butterscotch or chocolate sauce.

MINI CRUSTS

3 oz. cream cheese, softened   1 c. flour
½ c. margarine, softened

Combine and mix well. Chill dough. Shape into 24 balls. Place in ungreased miniature muffin tins and press dough against bottom and sides. Bake at 350°F. until golden brown.

Fill with pie filling of your choice or use to make Mini Quiche Lorraine.

EASY STRAWBERRY PIE

1 qt. fresh strawberries   1 (9 inch) baked pie crust
1½ c. confectioners sugar

Sprinkle ¼ cup powdered sugar in bottom of a pie crust. Place a layer of berries over the sugar, then sprinkle berries with more sugar. Add another layer of berries, then sprinkle with more sugar. Cover and refrigerate. Serves 6.

Optional: Top with whipped cream.

CHOCOLATE BANANA PIE

1 (3½ oz.) pkg. chocolate   2 to 3 sliced bananas
   pudding   1 baked pie crust

Prepare pudding according to package directions. Cool. Stir in sliced bananas. Pour into baked pie crust. Serves 6.

Optional: Top with meringue or whipped cream.

KAREN'S CHOCOLATE-PEANUT BUTTER TARTS

1 roll refrigerated ready-to-
   slice peanut butter
   cookie dough or sugar
   cookie dough

2 pkg. Reese's bite-size
   peanut butter cups
Melted butter

Slice cookie dough in 1 inch slices, then quarter the slices. Lay 1 piece in each *miniature muffin tin* (greased well with melted butter). Bake 8 minutes at 350°F. While cookies are hot and puffed, gently push a peanut butter cup into the center of each cookie. Cool; remove from tins. Keep refrigerated. Makes 32 to 36.

Variation: Use chocolate chip cookie dough.

MIRACLE PEANUT BUTTER COOKIES

1 c. chunky or extra chunky
   Peter Pan peanut
   butter

1 egg
1 c. sugar

Combine peanut butter, sugar, and egg. Mix well. Shape into balls. Flatten and crisscross with fork dipped in sugar. Bake on greased cookie sheet for 8 to 10 minutes at 375°F. Yield: 3 dozen.

Unbelievably delicious!

CHOCOLATE CHIP BARS

2 c. crushed graham crackers
1 c. chocolate chips

1 (14 oz.) can Eagle Brand
   sweetened milk

Combine and mix well all ingredients. Spread in a greased 9x9 inch pan. Bake at 350°F. for 20 to 25 minutes. Cut into bars. Serves 9 to 12.

PEANUT CLUSTERS

1½ lb. almond bark
1 (9 oz.) pkg. salted peanuts

1 (12 oz.) pkg. chocolate
   chips

Melt 1½ pounds almond bark and 12 ounces chocolate chips together in the top of a double boiler over boiling water. Stir constantly. When melted and smooth, stir in the peanuts. Drop by spoonfuls onto waxed paper. Let set until firm, or chill.

OREO COOKIE ICE CREAM

½ gal. vanilla ice cream,
   softened
12 oz. Cool Whip

1 small pkg. Oreo cookies,
   crushed

    Mix together and freeze in a 9x13 inch pan. Cut into squares to serve.
Serves 12.

FROZEN PEANUT BUTTER PIE

¾ c. chunky peanut butter
1 qt. vanilla ice cream,
   softened

1 graham cracker crust (or
   chocolate crust)

    Combine peanut butter and softened ice cream. Mix well. Pour into
your choice of pie crust and freeze. Serves 6 to 8.

ORANGE PINEAPPLE SHERBET

1 (20 oz.) can crushed
   pineapple (undrained)
1 large bottle Orange Crush
   (2 liter bottle)

2 cans (14 oz.) Eagle Brand
   sweetened milk

Combine and mix all ingredients. Freeze. Serves 8.

FORGOTTEN CHOCOLATE CHIP COOKIES

2 egg whites
⅔ c. sugar

1 c. chocolate chips

Beat egg whites until frothy. Add sugar and beat until stiff. Fold in chocolate chips. (Optional: Add pecans.) Preheat oven to 350°F. Drop teaspoons of mixture onto greased cookie sheet. Place in oven. *Turn off heat. Don't open door.* "Forget" the cookies until the next day.

GAIL WARD'S GRANDMOTHER'S SHORTBREAD

4 c. flour
2 c. butter (must be butter)

1 c. sugar

Gail's grandmother quoted her recipe as "twice as much flour as butter and twice as much butter as sugar." Cream the butter and all sugar, mixing well. Gradually work in flour. Mix with hands and knead 10 minutes until mixture holds together. Roll out ½ inch thick or pat on a breadboard. Cut into 1 inch squares. Prick the top with a fork. Bake on ungreased cookie sheets at 275°F. for 45 minutes or until lightly browned.

CHOCOLATE CHERRY DROPS

1 (6 oz.) pkg. chocolate chips
2 Tbsp. milk

1 (8 oz.) jar maraschino cherries, drained and sliced

In top of double boiler over hot water, melt chocolate chips. Stir in milk to make thick sauce. Add cherries and mix well. Drop by teaspoons onto waxed paper. Cool until firm.

ERNIE MASSEY'S HAYSTACKS

1½ c. cashews
1 large can chow mein
   noodles

1 (12 oz.) pkg. butterscotch
   chips

    Heat noodles and cashews in 250°F. oven to toast them. Stir often. Melt butterscotch chips and mix with chow mein noodles and cashews. Drop in clusters by teaspoonfuls onto waxed paper and let them set until firm. Makes about 3 dozen.

CHOCOLATE COVERED STRAWBERRIES

30 whole strawberries (with
   stems)

1 (12 oz.) pkg. chocolate
   chips
6 Tbsp. margarine

    Place clean berries on a large sheet of waxed paper which is setting on a cookie sheet. Melt chocolate chips in the top of a double boiler over hot water. Stir in margarine and mix until melted and blended with chocolate. Dip berries in chocolate, then replace on waxed paper and refrigerate until chocolate hardens.

STRAWBERRY SHERBET

9 (12 oz.) cans strawberry
   "pop"
3 (14 oz.) cans Eagle Brand
   milk

3 (10 oz.) pkg. frozen sliced
   strawberries

Combine, mix well, and freeze in a 6 quart freezer according to manufacturer's directions.

BRICKLE CHIP BROWNIES

1 box brownie mix
1 pkg. brickle chips (Heath
   Bits O' Brickle)

½ c. chopped pecans

Prepare brownie mix according to package directions. Stir in brickle chips and pecans. Bake as package directs. Serves 8.

CARROT CAKE

1 (18¼ oz.) box spice cake
   mix
2 c. shredded carrots

1 c. chopped black walnuts
   or pecans

    Prepare cake mix as package directs. Stir in carrots and nuts. Bake as package directs in a 9x13 inch pan that has been greased and floured. Cool before frosting. Serves 12.

    Note: Cream cheese frosting is good on this cake (recipe follows).

ICING FOR CARROT CAKE

1 (1 lb.) box powdered sugar
1 stick margarine, softened

1 (8 oz.) pkg. cream cheese,
   softened

    Combine margarine and cream cheese; beat until creamy. Stir in powdered sugar and beat. (Optional: Add 1 teaspoon vanilla.) Spread on Carrot Cake.

LEMON JELL-O CAKE

1 (18 oz.) pkg. yellow or
   lemon cake mix

1 large (6 oz.) pkg. lemon
   Jell-O
1 large ctn. Cool Whip
   topping

Mix cake according to directions on box and bake. Remove from oven, then poke holes in top of cake. Mix Jell-O, using 1 cup hot water only. When dissolved, pour Jell-O over cake and allow Jell-O to soak in. Let cake cool. Frost cake with Cool Whip. Serves 8 to 12.

MANDARIN LAYER CAKE

1 (18¼ oz.) box yellow cake
   mix
2 cans mandarin oranges,
   chopped and drained

¾ c. orange juice

Prepare cake mix as package directs, but add ¾ cup orange juice in place of ¾ cup of the liquid called for in the recipe. Stir in chopped oranges. Bake in 2 or 3 (8 inch) cake pans at 350°F. for 20 to 30 minutes. Cool and frost between layers, sides, and top. (Frosting recipe follows.) Serves 12.

FROSTING FOR MANDARIN ORANGE CAKE

1 large box instant vanilla
   pudding

1 (8 oz.) Cool Whip
1 (20 oz.) can crushed
   pineapple

Mix pudding and Cool Whip together. Drain pineapple partially and fold into Cool Whip and pudding mixture. Frost cooled cake.

CHRISTMAS FRUIT CAKE

1 (18¼ oz.) pkg. spice cake
   mix
1½ c. chopped candied fruit

1 c. pecan halves

Prepare spice cake according to directions on the box. Stir in candied fruit and pecans. Bake as directed on the package, adding 5 minutes more. Serves 12 to 16.

This cake looks especially nice if baked in a Bundt pan.

JANE BALLARD'S VANILLA ICE CREAM

2 (14 oz.) cans Eagle Brand   2 tsp. vanilla
  milk
6 c. milk

Combine, mix, and freeze in an ice cream freezer according to freezer directions. Makes 1½ gallons.

Note: Jane owns the Country Caboose Gift Shop in Joplin, Missouri. It's a great place to visit!

GINGERSNAPS

1 (14½ oz.) pkg. gingerbread   ⅓ c. oil
  mix
½ c. milk

Combine gingerbread mix, milk, and oil; beat with an electric mixer or by hand. Drop dough by teaspoonfuls onto a greased cookie sheet about 3 inches apart. Bake at 375°F. for 8 to 10 minutes. Remove cookies to rack to cool.

PECAN MACAROONS

2 eggs   16 oz. *finely ground pecans*
1 c. sugar

The nuts must be finely ground in a blender or food processor.

Beat eggs. Stir in sugar and mix well. Add pecans. Shape into balls. Place on a greased cookie sheet. Flatten balls with a fork. Bake at 350°F. for 12 to 15 minutes, or until lightly browned.

WALNUT CAKE

1 pkg. yellow cake mix   1 c. chopped black walnuts
1 c. pancake syrup

Prepare cake according to package directions. Stir in nuts and pour into a buttered 9x13 inch pan. Pour syrup over batter. Do not stir. Bake according to package directions.

Serve warm. Top with whipped cream, if desired. Serves 9.

ANGEL PUDDING CAKE

1 angel food cake, cubed
1 pkg. chocolate pudding

1 (8 to 12 oz.) container Cool
Whip topping

Place cake cubes in a greased 9x13 inch pan or glass Pyrex dish.

Prepare pudding according to package directions and spread over cake cubes.

Spread Cool Whip over pudding. Refrigerate 6 hours. Cut into squares to serve. Serves 9.

LEMON CHEESECAKE

1 (4 oz.) pkg. instant lemon
    pudding mix
1 graham cracker crust,
    baked

8 oz. Philadelphia cream
    cheese, softened

Prepare pudding as directed except blend cream cheese with milk before stirring into pudding. Pour into a baked crust and chill 2 to 4 hours. Serves 6.

ANN'S CHOCOLATE CHERRY CAKE

| 1 box Duncan Hines devils
 food cake mix | 1 (21 oz.) can cherry pie
 filling
2 eggs |

Combine and mix cake mix and eggs. Stir in cherry pie filling. Mix until well blended. Pour into a greased and floured 9x13 inch pan and bake for 35 to 40 minutes at 350°F.

For 2 (9 inch) cake pans, bake for 25 to 35 minutes. For Bundt pan, bake for 40 to 50 minutes.

Frost as desired. Serves 8.

RITZY CHOCOLATE COOKIES

| 1 box Ritz crackers
Chunky peanut butter | 1 (12 oz.) pkg. chocolate
 chips |

Spread a layer of peanut butter on each Ritz cracker.

Melt chocolate chips in top of a double boiler over boiling water. Stir until smooth.

Dip crackers in chocolate. Be sure to completely cover the peanut butter with chocolate. Lay on waxed paper to cool.

MACAROONS

1 (14 oz.) pkg. shredded
   coconut
1 (14 oz.) can Eagle Brand
   milk

1 tsp. vanilla

    Combine and mix all ingredients. Drop by spoonfuls onto a greased cookie sheet. Bake 8 minutes at 375°F. Cool before removing from pan. Makes about 3 dozen.

LEMON BARS

1 pkg. 1 step angel food cake
   mix
1 can lemon pie filling

Powdered sugar

    Combine cake mix and lemon pie filling; mix well. Pour into a greased jelly roll pan. Bake for 20 to 30 minutes at 350°. Sprinkle powdered sugar over it and cut into bars.

MARY SUTTON'S HAWAIIAN CAKE FROSTING

1 (3½ oz.) pkg. instant
   French vanilla pudding
   mix
1 (8 oz.) ctn. Cool Whip

1 (20 oz.) can crushed
   pineapple, drained

In a large bowl, combine pudding mix with pineapple and mix well. Stir in Cool Whip whipped topping. Let mixture stand on the cabinet for 15 minutes, then spread between layers and on top and sides of a pound cake.

Hint: Freeze a pound cake, then slice partially frozen cake into 4 layers horizontally. Frost cake. Refreeze cake. Slice to serve.

APPLE-SPICE CRISP

1 pkg. spice cake mix
1 can apple pie filling

1 stick margarine, sliced

Spread apple pie filling in a greased 9x13 inch dish. Sprinkle or spread dry spice cake mix over the fruit. Dot with slices of margarine (use more margarine if necessary). Bake at 350°F. for about 35 minutes, or until cake is browned.

CHILDREN'S CAKE CONES

1 (9 oz.) pkg. chocolate cake
    mix
1 (12 count) box ice cream
    cones (flat bottoms)

1 can cake frosting (your
    choice of flavors)

Prepare cake batter as package directs. Pour 3 tablespoons batter into ice cream cones, filling about half full. Set cones in muffin tins and bake for 25 to 30 minutes at 350°F. (These should rise to top of cone.) Cool. Frost with canned frosting.

CHOCOLATE COCONUT COOKIES

2 sq. Baker's chocolate
1 can moist flaked coconut

1 c. Eagle Brand milk

Heat together chocolate and milk; mix until smooth. Remove from heat and stir in coconut. Drop by teaspoonfuls onto a greased cookie sheet. Bake at 350°F. for 8 to 10 minutes.

CHOCOLATE COOKIES

1 pkg. chocolate cake mix
½ c. oil

2 eggs, beaten

Combine and mix well. (Optional: Stir in nuts.) Drop by teaspoonfuls onto greased cookie sheets. Bake at 325°F. for 12 to 15 minutes. Yield: 4 to 5 dozen cookies.

RICE KRISPIES BARS

½ lb. marshmallows
¼ c. oleo

5 c. Rice Krispies

Melt oleo and marshmallows in the top of a double boiler. Stir in cereal and mix well. Press into a buttered 9 inch square pan and cut into bars. Serves 9 to 12.

CHOCOLATE WALNUT DROPS

2 (1 oz.) sq. unsweetened
    chocolate
⅔ c. chopped black walnuts
    or pecans

1 (14 oz.) can Eagle Brand
    sweetened condensed
    milk

Melt chocolate squares in double boiler over hot water. Stir in milk until well blended. Mix in nuts. Drop mixture by teaspoonfuls onto a greased baking sheet. Bake at 350°F. for 12 to 15 minutes. Makes about 3 dozen.

MAMA COPELAND'S BANANA PUDDING DESSERT

1 box vanilla wafer cookies
1 (3½ oz.) pkg. banana
    pudding

4 to 6 sliced bananas

Prepare banana pudding according to package directions.

Make a cookie crust by placing whole cookies in bottom and along sides of a Pyrex dish.

Make layers of pudding, sliced bananas, and cookies. Repeat layers until all ingredients have been used. Refrigerate 2 to 4 hours to blend flavors. Serves 4.

APRICOT BALLS

½ lb. dried apricots, ground   ½ can Eagle Brand
2 c. coconut, shredded   sweetened milk

Combine, mix, and chill overnight. Shape into balls. Let set in covered container 1 day before eating.

CHOCOLATE-MARSHMALLOW CANDY

1 lb. milk chocolate   ½ c. chopped pecans or
1 c. miniature marshmallows   pecan halves

Melt chocolate in top of a double boiler. Line a 9x13 inch cake pan with waxed paper. Pour half of the melted chocolate over the waxed paper. Cover chocolate with marshmallows and nuts. Pour remaining half of the melted chocolate over it. Let cool completely, then break into pieces.

BUTTERSCOTCH BARS

1 (12 oz.) pkg. butterscotch
   morsels

1 c. chunky peanut butter
6 c. Rice Krispies cereal

     Combine butterscotch chips and peanut butter in a large saucepan; stir until smooth over low heat. Remove from heat and stir in Rice Krispies. Mix until well coated. Press into a buttered 9x13 inch pan. Chill until firm. Cut into squares.

STRAWBERRY ANGEL DELIGHT

2 (10 oz.) pkg. "Birds Eye"
   strawberry halves,
   thawed and drained

1 (3 oz.) pkg. strawberry jello
1 loaf size angel food cake,
   cubed

     Prepare jello according to package directions. Cut cake into 1 inch cubes and arrange one layer in a 9x9 inch Pyrex dish or glass bowl. When jello is partially jelled, stir in strawberries. Pour ½ of mixture over cake. Top with a second layer of cake cubes. Spread remaining jello over the top and refrigerate until firm.

S'MORES

Graham cracker squares
Hershey's chocolate squares

Marshmallows, partially
  melted

    Place graham cracker squares on a jelly roll pan. Top with a square of Hershey's chocolate. Lay a hot marshmallow over chocolate, then place a second cracker over marshmallow to form a sandwich.

CHOCOLATE CHEERIOS

2 c. chocolate chips
3 c. plain Cheerios

¾ c. chunky peanut butter

    Melt chocolate chips in double boiler. Mix in the peanut butter. Stir until smooth. Stir in Cheerios. Drop by spoonfuls onto waxed paper and let set until firm.

CHINESE NOODLE CANDY

1 (12 oz.) pkg. chocolate   ½ c. chopped pecans
   chips
1 can Chinese noodles

Melt chocolate. Stir in Chinese noodles and nuts. Drop by spoonfuls onto waxed paper. Let set until they are firm.

CHOCOLATE BANANA CREPES

4 bananas   1 can Hershey's chocolate
8 crepes   syrup

Split bananas lengthwise. Lay half of 1 banana in the middle of a crepe. Fold the crepe and drizzle chocolate syrup over it. Serves 8.

MRS. TRUMAN'S COCONUT BALLS

1 (7 oz.) pkg. shredded
   coconut
1 tsp. vanilla

⅔ c. Eagle Brand sweetened
   condensed milk

Combine the 3 ingredients and mix well. Shape into balls. Bake on greased cookie sheets for 15 minutes at 350°F. Yield: 3 dozen.

Note: Mrs. Truman served these at some White House gatherings.

LOUISE HOLTZINGER'S PEANUT BUTTER FUDGE

12 oz. chocolate chips
12 oz. peanut butter (extra
   chunky)

1 (14 oz.) can Eagle Brand
   sweetened condensed
   milk

Melt chocolate chips and peanut butter together in top of a double boiler over hot water. Remove from heat and stir in milk. Pour into an 8x8 inch pan lined with waxed paper and let it set until firm. Serves 8 to 12.

MARSHMALLOW FUDGE

1 (12 oz.) pkg. semi-sweet
   chocolate chips
1 (14 oz.) can Eagle Brand
   condensed milk

6 to 8 oz. miniature
   marshmallows

Melt chocolate chips in microwave or in top of a double boiler. Remove from heat and stir until creamy. Mix in Eagle Brand milk, then the marshmallows. Pour into a buttered pan. Cool, then refrigerate until firm. Cut into squares.

THELMA PRUITT'S STRAWBERRY CANDY

2 (6 oz.) pkg. strawberry Jell-
   O (dry)

1 (14 oz.) can Eagle Brand
   milk
1 (8 oz.) pkg. flaked coconut

Combine and mix well. Refrigerate overnight. Shape into strawberry-size balls. (Optional: Roll in sugar.) Keep refrigerated.

Note: I have 2 recipes for this recipe. One calls for one 3 ounce can coconut and the other calls for one 8 ounce package shredded coconut. Use whichever measurement you prefer. I used 8 ounces coconut when I made them.

MINCEMEAT SQUARES

1⅓ c. None Such mincemeat
**1 (14 oz.) can Eagle Brand
milk**

2 c. graham cracker crumbs

Combine and mix together. Spread in a greased 9x13 inch pan and bake at 350°F. for 35 to 40 minutes. Cool before cutting into squares.

Optional: Stir in ½ cup chopped pecans or sprinkle on top of batter before baking.

LOWFAT FUDGE BROWNIES

1 box lite fudge brownie mix
**5.5 oz. Hershey's chocolate
syrup**

½ c. Egg Beaters

Combine all ingredients in a large mixing bowl and mix until moistened. If mixture is too dry, add a little water, 1 tablespoon at a time. Spray a 9x13 inch glass baking dish with nonfat cooking spray. Pour mixture into pan and bake at 350°F. for 25 to 30 minutes. Cool. Yield: 36 squares.

Contains 1½ grams fat per piece.

BETTY KOLBE'S CHOCOLATE
APPLESAUCE CAKE

1 box lowfat chocolate cake
   mix
1 (16 oz.) can applesauce

½ to ¾ c. Egg Beaters egg
   substitute

Combine the 3 ingredients in a mixing bowl and mix until well-blended. Pour into a 9x13 inch pan that was sprayed with a nonfat cooking spray. Bake as package directs. Serves 12 to 16.

Contains less than ½ fat gram per serving.

CANDY APPLES

1 lb. caramels
2 Tbsp. margarine

5 to 6 Red Delicious apples

Remove stems from apples; wash and dry. Melt caramels and margarine in top of double boiler. Stir until smooth. Push a wooden popsicle stick into each apple's stem end. Dip each apple into the caramel sauce, covering completely. Lay apples on waxed paper until they have dried and caramel has hardened.

BUTTERSCOTCH FLAKES

1 (6 oz.) pkg. butterscotch
  chips
2 or 3 c. corn flakes

½ c. peanut butter

    Melt chips and peanut butter in a double boiler; mix well. Remove from heat and stir in corn flakes. Drop by teaspoonfuls onto waxed paper. Let set until they harden.

DICK HADER'S MAPLE FUDGE

1½ c. dark Karo syrup
6 c. sugar

3 (½ pt.) ctn. whipping cream

    Combine, mix, and cook all ingredients in a large pan or skillet to soft ball stage. Remove from heat. Beat with electric mixer until smooth and stiff. Pour onto pan and let set until firm. Cut into squares.

FUDGE SAUCE

1 c. Milnot   **1 (6 oz.) pkg. chocolate chips**
1 c. miniature marshmallows

Combine Milnot, marshmallows, and chocolate chips in a saucepan; stir until melted.

This is good served over ice cream or over Peanut Butter Ice Cream Pie.

LOIS DAVIS' CHOCOLATE COVERED PRETZELS

1 lb. white almond bark,   **¼ tsp. vanilla flavoring**
melted
Pretzels

Melt almond bark and stir in flavoring. Dip pretzels in melted almond bark. Place on waxed paper to dry.

LUCY WORNALL'S COCOA PUFF CANDY

1½ lb. white chocolate
4½ c. Cocoa Puffs cereal

1 (12 oz.) can Planters red
   skin peanuts

    Melt chocolate. Stir in cereal and peanuts. Drop by teaspoonfuls onto waxed paper. Let set until candy is firm.

JUDITH'S ALMOND MACAROONS

1 (8 oz.) can Solo brand
   almond paste
⅔ c. granulated sugar

¼ c. egg whites (from 2 to 3
   eggs)

    In a mixing bowl, cut almond paste into small pieces. Blend with sugar. Add egg whites and beat for 4 to 5 minutes or until mixture is smooth. Drop by tablespoons onto baking sheets lined with brown paper. Leave about 1 inch space between each cookie. Bake at 350°F. for 18 to 20 minutes or until golden brown. Cool 5 minutes in pan. Remove from pan and cool on wire rack. Yields 2 dozen half dollar size cookies.

    Hint: If cookies stick, dampen the back of the paper with a moist cloth. After a few minutes, remove cookies from the paper.

CHOCOLATE PEANUT BUTTER CUPS

1 (21.5 oz.) pkg. Duncan
    Hines double fudge
    brownie mix
2 (9 oz.) pkg. miniature
    peanut butter cups

2 eggs

Prepare brownie mix according to directions, using 2 eggs. Spoon into miniature foil cupcake liners, filling ¾ full. Place peanut butter cup in center of each and push into batter. Preheat oven to 350°F. and bake for 20 to 25 minutes or until cake tests done.

NANCY REAGAN'S LEMON DESSERT

4 lemons
Mint

Lemon sherbet

Cut off bottoms of lemons so they will stand firmly on a plate. Slice ½ inch off the top. Save this cap. Scoop out lemon and juice. Fill lemon shells with lemon sherbet. Place cap of lemon back on top, plus a sprig of mint. Serves 8.

SHAKER BOILED APPLES

6 red cooking apples, cored   **½ c. sugar**
Cold water

Place apples in a large saucepan. Add ½ inch cold water. Pour sugar over apples. Boil gently 20 minutes or until apples are tender. Turn apples over several times and stir until the sugar and water form a syrup.

Serve syrup in a small pitcher along with apples and pour syrup over apples. Serves 6.

CHOCOLATE SYRUP

1 c. cocoa   **2 c. hot water**
2 c. sugar

Mix cocoa and sugar. Add a little water to make a paste. Add remaining water and bring to a boil. Boil for 1 minute. Pour into a jar and cover with a lid.

To serve as a beverage, add 1 part syrup to 4 or 5 parts milk and mix well.

Serve over frozen nonfat yogurt for a sundae or stir into a Coca-Cola for a chocolate Coke.

GAIL WARD'S GRAHAM CRACKER TREATS

24 graham crackers
1 c. brown sugar

1 c. butter or margarine

Break graham crackers into halves at perforations. Line 10x17 inch baking pan with foil. Arrange crackers in the prepared pan.

Combine butter and brown sugar in saucepan. Heat. Boil for 2 minutes until bubbly.

Spread sugar mixture over crackers. Bake at 375°F. for 8 minutes or until bubbly.

Optional: Sprinkle with nuts before baking.

BROWNIE DROP COOKIES

1 pkg. fudge brownie mix
¼ c. water

1 egg

Combine the 3 ingredients in a bowl and mix well. Dough will be stiff. Drop by teaspoonfuls onto lightly greased baking sheet. Bake for 6 to 8 minutes at 375°F. Cool slightly before removing from the cookie sheet. Yield: 3 to 4 dozen.

VELORA HOLT'S MARSHMALLOW DROPS

2 c. Rice Krispies cereal
1 c. marshmallow cream

½ c. raisins

Heat marshmallow cream in top of a double boiler until syrupy. Remove from heat. Pour over cereal and raisins and mix well. Drop by teaspoonfuls onto aluminum foil. Refrigerate until firm. Yield: 3 dozen. *Fat free.*

Optional: Use corn flakes instead of Rice Krispies for a different taste.

VIRGINIA NASH'S PINK PEPPERMINT ICE CREAM

1 qt. milk
1 lb. peppermint sticks,
**   chopped**

1 qt. cream

Drop chopped candy in milk. Cover and refrigerate overnight. Next day, pour into an ice cream freezer. Stir in cream. Freeze.

Variation: Try hard peppermint candies instead of peppermint sticks.

CHOCOLATE ICE CREAM

1 (14 oz.) can Eagle Brand
    condensed milk
1 large container Cool Whip
    whipped cream

1 gal. chocolate milk

Fold condensed milk and Cool Whip into 1 quart of chocolate milk. Pour into freezer container. Add remaining chocolate milk to the "fill line," then freeze according to directions.

PINEAPPLE CAKE

1 (20 oz.) can pineapple
    (crushed)

2 sticks margarine, sliced
1 box white or yellow cake
    mix

Spread pineapple in a greased 9x13 inch dish. Sprinkle dry cake mix over the fruit. Dot with slices of oleo. Bake at 350°F. for about 35 minutes or until browned. Serves 6 to 8.

Optional: Top with a dip of vanilla ice cream.

Notes

Miscellaneous

TEMPERATURE TESTS
FOR CANDY MAKING

There are two different methods of determining when candy has been cooked to the proper consistency. One is by using a candy thermometer in order to record degrees, the other is by using the cold water test. The chart below will prove useful in helping to follow candy recipes:

TYPE OF CANDY	DEGREES	COLD WATER
Fondant, Fudge	234 - 238°	Soft Ball
Divinity, Caramels	245 - 248°	Firm Ball
Taffy	265 - 270°	Hard Ball
Butterscotch	275 - 280°	Light Crack
Peanut Brittle	285 - 290°	Hard Crack
Caramelized Sugar	310 - 321°	Caramelized

In using the cold water test, use a fresh cupful of cold water for each test. When testing, remove the candy from the fire and pour about ½ teaspoon of candy into the cold water. Pick the candy up in the fingers and roll into a ball if possible.

In the SOFT BALL TEST the candy will roll into a soft ball which quickly loses its shape when removed from the water.

In the FIRM BALL TEST the candy will roll into a firm, but not hard ball. It will flatten out a few minutes after being removed from the water.

In the HARD BALL TEST the candy will roll into a hard ball which has lost almost all plasticity and will roll around on a plate on removal from the water.

In the LIGHT CRACK TEST the candy will form brittle threads which will soften on removal from the water.

In the HARD CRACK TEST the candy will form brittle threads in the water which will remain brittle after being removed from the water.

In CARAMELIZING the sugar first melts then becomes a golden brown. It will form a hard brittle ball in cold water.

MISCELLANEOUS

MICROWAVE FUDGE

1 (12 oz.) pkg. chocolate
   chips
1 tsp. vanilla

1 (14 oz.) can Eagle Brand
   condensed milk

Combine chocolate chips and milk in a glass dish and microwave on HIGH for 3 minutes. Stir until melted and smooth. Mix in the vanilla. (Optional: Add 1 cup chopped black walnuts or pecans.)

Spread evenly into a foil-lined 8 inch square pan and chill until firm. Cut into squares.

LOBSTER TAILS

4 (8 oz.) frozen lobster tails
2 Tbsp. butter

1 Tbsp. lemon juice

Microwave butter in a small bowl at HIGH until melted. Add lemon juice to melted butter and brush mixture onto lobster tail meat. Face tails shell-side down in baking dish. Cover with waxed paper and microwave on HIGH for 6 to 10 minutes, turning every 3 minutes.

Serve with additional melted butter, if desired. Serves 4.

VELORA HOLT'S COLE SLAW DRESSING

1 c. mayonnaise (*not* salad
   dressing)
½ c. sugar

¼ c. vinegar

    Combine and mix until well blended. Refrigerate. Serve over Cole Slaw Salad or Waldorf Salad.

DESSIE CARMACK'S FROZEN STRAWBERRY JAM

4 c. mashed strawberries
2 pkg. Sure-Jell

8 c. sugar

    Mix sugar and berries. Let stand 20 minutes. Stir 3 to 4 times.

    Mix Sure-Jell with 2 cups water. Bring to boil for 1 minute. Remove from stove. Stir in berry-sugar mixture. Stir 5 minutes. Pour into sterilized glass jars. Let stand 2 days at room temperature. Tighten lids and freeze. (Spread on toast or can be poured over ice cream.

EGG SUBSTITUTE

3 egg whites
1 tsp. vegetable oil

3 drops of yellow food color

Combine egg whites and food color. Mix in oil; cover and refrigerate. This should be used within 2 days.

This amount makes ½ cup egg substitute and equals 2 whole eggs. It can be used in any recipe calling for 2 eggs.

MYRTLE HULL'S WHITE SAUCE (MEDIUM)

4 Tbsp. butter or margarine
4 Tbsp. flour

2 c. milk

Melt margarine in saucepan. Add flour and mix well. Remove from heat. Gradually stir in milk and return to heat. Cook, stirring constantly, until thickened and smooth. Makes 2 cups.

SWEETENED CONDENSED MILK

1 c. plus 2 Tbsp. instant   ½ c. warm water
   nonfat dry milk   ¾ c. sugar

Combine dry milk and warm water; mix well. Set mixing container in a pan of hot water and stir in ¾ cup sugar. Stir until sugar is dissolved. Chill until thickened.

This equals 1 (8 ounce) cup of Eagle Brand sweetened condensed milk.

"TONIC" FOR HEALTHY PLANTS

1 env. Knox unflavored   3 c. cold water
   gelatine
1 c. hot water

Dissolve gelatine in 1 cup hot water. Mix well. Stir in 3 cups cold water. Pour into jar with tight lid. Use once monthly on your plants. They will be healthier and greener. Yield: 4 cups.

Notes

Notes

INDEX OF RECIPES

MISCELLANEOUS

KITCHEN HINTS

If you've over-salted soup or vegetables, add cut raw potatoes and discard once they have cooked and absorbed the salt.

A teaspoon each of cider vinegar and sugar added to salty soup or vegetables will also remedy the situation.

If you've over-sweetened a dish, add salt.

A teaspoon of cider vinegar will take care of too-sweet vegetable or main dishes.

Pale gravy may be browned by adding a bit of instant coffee straight from the jar . . . no bitter taste, either.

If you will brown the flour well before adding to the liquid when making gravy, you will avoid pale or lumpy gravy.

A different way of browning flour is to put it in a custard cup placed beside meat in the oven. Once the meat is done, the flour will be nice and brown.

Thin gravy can be thickened by adding a mixture of flour or cornstarch and water, which has been mixed to a smooth paste, added gradually, stirring constantly, while bringing to a boil.

Lumpless gravy can be your triumph if you add a pinch of salt to the flour before mixing it with water.

A small amount of baking soda added to gravy will eliminate excess grease.

Drop a lettuce leaf into a pot of homemade soup to absorb excess grease from the top.

If time allows, the best method of removing fat is refrigeration until the fat hardens. If you put a piece of waxed paper over the top of the soup, etc. it can be peeled right off, along with the hardened fat.

Ice cubes will also eliminate the fat from soup and stew. Just drop a few into the pot and stir; the fat will cling to the cubes; discard the cubes before they melt. Or, wrap ice cubes in paper towel or cheesecloth and skim over the top.

If fresh vegetables are wilted or blemished, pick off the brown edges, sprinkle with cool water, wrap in paper towel and refrigerate for an hour or so.

Perk up soggy lettuce by adding lemon juice to a bowl of cold water and soak for an hour in the refrigerator.

Lettuce and celery keep longer if you store them in paper bags instead of cellophane.

To remove the core from a head of lettuce, hit the core end once against the counter sharply. The core will loosen and pull out easily.

Cream will whip faster and better if you'll first chill the cream, bowl, and beaters well.

Soupy whipped cream can be saved by adding an egg white, then chilling thoroughly. Re-beat for a fluffy surprise!

A few drops of lemon juice added to whipping cream helps it whip faster and better.

Cream whipped ahead of time will not separate if you add ¼ teaspoon unflavored gelatin per cup of cream.

A dampened and folded dish towel placed under the bowl in which you are whipping cream will keep the bowl from dancing all over the counter top.

Brown sugar won't harden if an apple slice is placed in the container.

But if your brown sugar is already brick-hard, put your cheese-grater to work and grate the amount you need.

KITCHEN HINTS

A slice of soft bread placed in the package of hardened brown sugar will soften it again in a couple of hours.

Potatoes will bake in a hurry if they are boiled in salted water for 10 minutes before popping into a very hot oven.

A leftover baked potato can be rebaked if you dip it in water and bake in a 350° oven for about 20 minutes.

A thin slice cut from each end of the potato will speed up baking time as well.

You'll shed less tears if you'll cut the root end off of the onion last.

No more tears when peeling onions if you place them in the deep freeze for four or five minutes first.

Scalding tomatoes, peaches, or pears in boiling water before peeling makes it easier on you and the fruit — skins slip right off.

Ripen green fruits by placing in a perforated plastic bag. The holes allow air movement, yet retain the odorless gas which fruits produce to promote ripening.

To hasten the ripening of garden tomatoes or avocados, put them in a brown paper bag, close the bag and leave at room temperature for a few days.

When pan frying always heat the pan before adding the butter or oil.

A little salt sprinkled into the frying pan will prevent spattering.

Meat loaf will not stick if you place a slice of bacon on the bottom of the pan.

Vinegar brought to a boil in a new frying pan will prevent foods from sticking.

Muffins will slide right out of tin pans if the hot pan is first placed on a wet towel.

No sticking to the pan when you're scalding milk if you'll first rinse the pan in cold water.

Add a cup of water to the bottom portion of the broiling pan before sliding into the oven, to absorb smoke and grease.

A few teaspoons of sugar and cinnamon slowly burned on top of the stove will hide unpleasant cooking odors and make your family think you've been baking all day!

A lump of butter or a few teaspoons of cooking oil added to water when boiling rice, noodles, or spaghetti will prevent boiling over.

Rubbing the inside of the cooking vessel with vegetable oil will also prevent noodles, spaghetti, and similar starches from boiling over.

A few drops of lemon juice added to simmering rice will keep the grains separate.

Grating a stick of butter softens it quickly.

Soften butter for spreading by inverting a small heated pan over the butter dish for a while.

A dip of the spoon or cup into hot water before measuring shortening or butter will cause the fat to slip out easily without sticking to the spoon.

Before measuring honey or other syrup, oil the cup with cooking oil and rinse in hot water.

Catsup will flow out of the bottle evenly if you will first insert a drinking straw, push it to the bottom of the bottle, and remove.

If you wet the dish on which the gelatin is to be unmolded, it can be moved around until centered.

KITCHEN HINTS

A dampened paper towel or terry cloth brushed downward on a cob of corn will remove every strand of corn silk.

An easy way to remove the kernels of sweet corn from the cob is to use a shoe horn. It's built just right for shearing off those kernels in a jiffy.

To determine whether an egg is fresh, immerse it in a pan of cool, salted water. If it sinks, it is fresh; if it rises to the surface, throw it away.

Fresh eggs' shells are rough and chalky; old eggs are smooth and shiny.

To determine whether an egg is hard-boiled, spin it. If it spins, it is hard-boiled; if it wobbles and will not spin it is raw.

Egg whites won't run while boiling or poaching if you'll add a little vinegar to the water.

Eggs will beat up fluffier if they are allowed to come to cool room temperature before beating.

For baking, it's best to use medium to large eggs; extra large eggs may cause cakes to fall when cooled.

Egg shells can be easily removed from hard-boiled eggs if they are quickly rinsed in cold water first.

For fluffier omelets, add a pinch of cornstarch before beating.

For a never fail, never weep meringue, add a teaspoon of cornstarch to the sugar before beating it into the egg whites.

Once your meringue is baked, cut it cleanly, using a knife coated with butter.

A meringue pie may be covered with waxed paper or plastic wrap with no fear of sticking, if you'll first grease the paper with oleo.

No "curly" bacon for breakfast when you dip it into cold water before frying.

Keep bacon slices from sticking together; roll the package into a tube shape and secure with rubber bands.

A quick way to separate frozen bacon: heat a spatula over a burner, slide it under each slice to separate it from the others.

Cheese won't harden if you'll butter the exposed edges before storing.

A cloth dampened with vinegar and wrapped around cheese will also prevent drying out.

Thaw fish in milk. The milk draws out the frozen taste and provides a fresh-caught flavor.

When browning any piece of meat, the job will be done more quickly and effectively if the meat is very dry and the fat is very hot.

You'll get more juice from a lemon if you'll first warm it slightly in the oven.

Popcorn will stay fresh and you will eliminate "old maids" if you store it in the freezer.

Running ice cold water over the kernels before popping will also eliminate "old maids".

After flouring chicken, chill for one hour. The coating adheres better during frying.

Empty salt cartons with spouts make dandy containers for bread crumbs. A funnel is used for getting the crumbs into the carton.

A sack of lumpy sugar won't be if you place it in the refrigerator for 24 hours.

CLEANUPS

Fill blender part way with hot water; add a drop of detergent; cover and turn it on for a few seconds. Rinse and drain dry.

Loosen grime from can openers by brushing with an old toothbrush. To clean blades, run a paper towel through the cutting process.

Don't panic if you accidentally scorch the inside of your favorite saucepan. Just fill the pan halfway with water and add ¼ cup baking soda. Boil awhile until the burned portions loosen and float to the top.

A jar lid or a couple of marbles in the bottom half of a double-boiler will rattle when the water gets low and warn you to add more before the pan scorches or burns.

To remove lime deposits from teakettles, fill with equal parts vinegar and water. Bring to a boil and allow to stand overnight.

Before washing fine china and crystal, place a towel in the bottom of the sink to act as a cushion.

To remove coffee or tea stains and cigarette burns from fine china, rub with a damp cloth dipped in baking soda.

To quickly remove food that is stuck to a casserole dish, fill with boiling water and 2 tablespoons of baking soda or salt.

To clear a sink or basin drain, pour ½ cup of baking soda followed by a cup of vinegar down the drain . . .let the mixture foam, then run hot water.

When a drain is clogged with grease, pour a cup of salt and a cup of baking soda followed by a kettle of boiling water.

Silver will gleam after a rubbing with damp baking soda on a soft cloth.

For a fast and simple clean-up of your hand grater, rub salad oil on the grater before using.

A toothbrush works great to clean lemon rind, cheese, onion, etc. out of the grater before washing it.

While baking fruit pies, does the juice runneth over? Shake salt into the spills. They'll burn to a crisp and can be easily scraped up with a spatula.

Grease splatters or other foods that have dried on the stove, burner rings, counter appliances, etc., may be removed by applying dry baking soda to the spots, then rubbing with a damp cloth. Rinse with clear water, dry and enjoy the like-new look.

CALORIE COUNTER

Almonds:
roasted in oil, salted, 9-10 nuts 62
Apple butter, 1 tbsp. 33
Apple juice, canned or bottled, 1 cup 117
Apples:
fresh, with skin, 1 average (2½" diameter) 61
dried, cooked, sweetened, ½ cup 157
dried, cooked, unsweetened, ½ cup 100
Applesauce, canned, sweetened, ½ cup 116
Applesauce, canned, unsweetened, ½ cup 50
Apricot nectar, canned or bottled, 1 cup 143
Apricots:
fresh, 3 average (12 per lb.) 55
canned, 4 halves with 2 tbsp. heavy syrup 105
canned, water pack, ½ cup with liquid 38
Asparagus:
canned, drained, cut spears, ½ cup 25
frozen, 6 spears 23
Avocados, 3⅛" diameter 185

Bacon, fried, drained, 2 medium slices 86
Bacon, Canadian, fried, drained, 1 slice 58
Bagel, egg or water, 1 medium (3" diameter) 165
Bamboo shoots, raw, cuts, ½ cup 21
Bananas, 1 average 118
Bean sprouts, soy, raw, ½ cup 24
Beans, baked, canned:
with pork and tomato sauce, ½ cup 156
Beans, green or snap:
fresh, boiled, drained, cuts or French style, ½ cup . . 16
canned, with liquid, ½ cup 22
Beans, lima, immature seeds:
boiled, drained, ½ cup 95
canned, with liquid, ½ cup 88
Beans, pea, navy, or white, dry, cooked, ½ cup 112
Beans, red kidney, canned, with liquid, ½ cup 115
Beef, choice grade cuts (without bone):
brisket, lean only, braised, 4 oz. 253
chuck, arm, lean only, pot-roasted, 4 oz. 219
club steak, lean only, broiled, 4 oz. 277
flank steak, lean only, pot-roasted, 4 oz. 222
ground, lean (10% fat), broiled, 4 oz. 248
porterhouse steak, lean only, broiled, 4 oz. 254
rib, lean only, roasted, 4 oz. 273
round steak, lean only, broiled, 4 oz. 214
rump, lean only, roasted, 4 oz. 236
short plate, lean only, simmered, 4 oz. 253
sirloin steak, double-bone, lean only, broiled, 4 oz. . 245
sirloin steak, round-bone, lean only, broiled, 4 oz. . 235
T-bone steak, lean only, broiled, 4 oz. 253
Beef, corned:
boiled, medium-fat, 4 oz. 422
canned, lean, 4 oz. 211
Beef and vegetable stew, canned, 4 oz. 90
Beets:
boiled, drained, sliced, ½ cup 33
Blackberries:
fresh, ½ cup 42
canned, juice pack, ½ cup with liquid 68
Blueberries:
fresh, ½ cup 45
canned, water pack, ½ cup with liquid 47
Bologna, all meat, 4 oz. 315
Boysenberries:
canned, water pack, ½ cup with liquid 45
frozen, unsweetened, ½ cup 30
Braunschweiger (smoked liverwurst), 4 oz. 362
Brazil nuts (3 large nuts) 90
Bread, commercial:
Boston brown, 1 slice 101
cracked wheat, 1 slice, 20 per loaf 60
French, 1 slice 44
Italian, 1 slice 28

pumpernickel, 1 slice 79
raisin, 1 slice, 20 per loaf 60
rye, light, 1 slice, 20 per loaf 56
white, firm-crumb type, 1 slice, 20 per loaf 63
whole wheat, firm-crumb type, 1 slice, 20 per loaf . . 56
Bread stuffing, mix, mixed with butter, water, ½ cup . 250
Broccoli:
raw, 1 large spear 32
boiled, drained, cut spears, ½ cup 20
Brussels sprouts boiled, drained ½ cup 28
Butter, 1 Tbsp. 100
Butter, whipped, 1 tbsp. 67

Cabbage:
red, raw, chopped or shredded, ½ cup 14
white, raw, chopped or shredded, ½ cup 11
Cake, mix, prepared as directed on package:
angelfood, without icing, 3½-oz. serving 269
coffee cake, 3½-oz. serving 322
devil's food, with chocolate icing, 3½-oz. serving . . 369
white, with chocolate icing, 3½-oz. serving 351
yellow, with chocolate icing, 3½-oz. serving 365
Candies, 1-oz. serving:
almonds, chocolate-covered 161
butter mints, after dinner (Kraft) 106
butterscotch 112
cherries, dark chocolate-covered (Welch's) 115
chocolate, milk 147
chocolate, semi-sweet 144
coconut, chocolate-covered 124
fudge, chocolate, with nuts 121
gum drops 98
jelly beans 104
licorice (Switzer) 101
Life Savers, all flavors except mint 111
Life Savers, mint 108
mints, chocolate-covered 116
marshmallows (Campfire) 100
peanut brittle 119
peanut cluster, chocolate-covered (Kraft) 151
raisins, chocolate-covered 120
toffee, chocolate (Kraft) 111
Cantaloupe, fresh, ½ melon, 5" diameter 58
Carrots:
raw, 1 average 21
boiled, drained, diced, ½ cup 23
Catsup, tomato, bottled, 1 tbsp. 16
Cauliflower:
raw, flowerbuds, sliced, ½ cup 12
boiled, drained, flowerbuds, ½ cup 14
Celery, raw, 1 outer stalk (8" long) 7
Cereals:
All-bran, 1 cup 192
bran, 100% (Nabisco), 1 cup 150
bran flakes, 40%, 1 cup 106
bran flakes with raisins, 1 cup 144
corn flakes, 1 cup 97
corn flakes, sugar coated, 1 cup 154
Cream of Wheat, cooked, 1 cup 133
farina, quick-cooking, cooked, 1 cup 105
oat flakes (Post), 1 cup 165
oatmeal or rolled oats, cooked, 1 cup 132
rice, puffed, 1 cup 60
wheat flakes, 1 cup 106
wheat, puffed, 1 cup 54
wheat, puffed, presweetened, 1 cup 132
wheat, shredded, 1 biscuit (2½" x 2" x 1¼") 89
Cheese:
American, processed, 1 oz. 105
blue or Roquefort type, 1 oz. 104
brick, 1 oz. 105
cheddar, domestic, 1 oz. 113
cottage, creamed, small curd, ½ cup 112

CALORIE COUNTER

cream, 1 tbsp. 52
cream, whipped, 1 tbsp. 37
Gouda, 1 oz. 108
Monterey Jack, 1 oz. 103
Mozzarella, part-skim, 1 oz. 85
Muenster, 1 oz. 100
Neufchatel (Borden's), 1 oz. 73
Old English, processed, 1 oz. 105
Parmesan, grated, 1 Tbsp. 23
pimiento, American, processed, 1 oz. 105
Provolone, 1 oz. 99
ricotta, moist, 1 oz. 45
Romano, 1 oz. 110
Roquefort, 1 oz. 105
Swiss, domestic, 1 oz. 104
Cheese food, American, processed, 1 oz. 92
Cherries:
sweet, fresh, whole, ½ cup 41
Cherries, maraschino, bottled, 1 oz. with liquid 33
Chestnuts, fresh, 10 average 141
Chicken:
broiled, meat only, 4 oz. 154
roasted, dark meat, 4 oz., no skin 204
roasted, light meat, 4 oz., no skin 207
Chili, with beans, canned ½ cup 170
Chili, without beans, canned, ½ cup 255
Coconut:
dried, sweetened, shredded, ½ cup 258
Cod (meat only):
broiled, with butter, fillets, 4 oz. 192
frozen, fish sticks, breaded, 5 sticks, 4 oz. 276
Coffee, prepared, plain, 1 cup 2
Coleslaw, commercial, with mayonnaise, ½ cup 87
Cookies, commercial:
brownies, from mix, with nuts and water, 1 oz. . . . 114
butter thins, 1 piece (2" diameter) 23
chocolate chip, 1 piece (2¼" diameter) 50
coconut bar, 1 oz. 140
fig bar, 1 average piece 50
gingersnaps, 1 piece (2" diameter) 29
graham cracker, plain, 1 piece (5" x 2½") 55
ladyfinger, 1 piece 40
macaroon, 1 piece (2¾" diameter) 91
oatmeal with raisins, 1 piece (2⅝" diameter) 59
peanut sandwich, 1 piece (1¾" diameter) 58
shortbread, 1 average piece 37
vanilla wafer, 1 piece (1¾" diameter) 19
Corn:
boiled, drained on cob, 1 ear (5" x 1¾") 70
boiled, drained, kernels, ½ cup 69
canned, cream style, ½ cup 105
Corn chips (Fritos), 1 oz. 166
Crackers:
bacon-flavor, 1 oz. 127
butter, round, 1 piece (1⅞" diameter) 15
cheese, round, 1 piece (1⅝" diameter) 17
Melba toast, white, regular, 1 piece 15
Rye-Krisp, 1 piece (1⅞" x 3½") 21
saltines, 1 piece 12
whole wheat, 1 oz. 114
Cranberry juice cocktail, canned or bottled, 1 cup . . . 164
Cranberry sauce, canned, strained, ½ cup 202
Cream:
half and half, ½ cup 162
sour, 1 tbsp. 26
whipping, light, ½ cup unwhipped 358
whipping, heavy, ½ cup, unwhipped 419
Cream substitute, non-dairy, dry, 1 tbsp. 33
Cucumber, with skin, 1 large (8¼" long) 45

Dates, domestic, 10 average 219
Duck, domestic, roasted, meat only, 4 oz. 352

Eclair, custard filled, with chocolate icing, 1 average . 239
Eggnog, 8% fat (Borden's), ½ cup 171
Eggplant, boiled, drained, diced, ½ cup 19
Eggs, chicken:
boiled or poached, 1 large egg 82
fried, with 1 tsp. butter, 1 large egg 99
scrambled, with 1 tsp. butter, 1 large egg 111
Endive, raw, 10 small leaves 5
Escarole, raw, 1 large leaf 4

Fat, vegetable shortening, 1 tbsp. 111
Figs:
dried, 1 large fig (2" x 1") 57
Fish cakes, fried, frozen, reheated, 4 oz. 306
Flour:
all-purpose, sifted, 1 cup 419
buckwheat, dark, sifted, 1 cup 326
cake or pastry, sifted, 1 cup 349
rye, dark, sifted, 1 cup 419
wheat, self-rising, sifted, 1 cup 405
Frankfurters, all-meat, 1 average (10 per lb.) 133
Fruit cocktail, canned, water pack, ½ cup with liquid . . 46
Fruit, mixed, frozen, sweetened, 4 oz. 125

Gelatin dessert, flavored, prepared with water, ½ cup . 71
Gooseberries, fresh, ½ cup 30
Grape drink, canned, 1 cup 135
Grape juice, canned or bottled, 1 cup 167
Grapes:
fresh (Concord, Delaware, etc.), 10 18
fresh (Thompson seedless, etc.), 10 34
Grapefruit juice:
canned, sweetened, 1 cup 133
canned, unsweetened, 1 cup 101

Haddock, fried, breaded fillets, 4 oz. 187
Halibut, fillets, broiled with butter, 4 oz. 194
Halibut, frozen, steak, 4 oz. 254
Halibut, smoked, 4 oz. 254
Ham:
boiled, packaged, 4 oz. (about 4 slices) 266
fresh, medium-fat, roasted, 4 oz. 426
picnic, cured, medium-fat, roasted, 4 oz. 368
canned, cured, lean only, roasted, 4 oz. 241
canned, deviled, 4 oz. 398
Herring:
canned, plain, 4 oz. with liquid 236
pickled, Bismark-type, 4 oz. 253
smoked, hard, 4 oz. 340
Hickory nuts, shelled, 4 oz. 763
Honey, strained or extracted, 1 tbsp. 64
Honeydew melon:
fresh, 1 wedge (2" x 7") 49

Ice cream:
hardened, rich, 16% fat, ½ cup 165
soft-serve (frozen custard), ½ cup 167
Ice cream bar, chocolate coated, 3-oz. bar 162
Ice cream cone, sugar 1 cone 37
Ice cream cone, waffle, 1 cone 19
Ice milk, hardened, 5.1% fat, ½ cup 100
Ice milk, soft-serve, 5.1% fat, ½ cup 133
Ice milk bar, chocolate coated, 3-oz. bar 144

Jams and preserves, all flavors, 1 tbsp. 54
Jellies, all flavors, 1 tbsp. 49

Kale:
fresh, leaves only, 4 oz. 80
fresh, with stems, boiled, drained, ½ cup 16
Knockwurst, 1 link (4" x 1⅛" diameter) 189
Kumquats, fresh, 1 average 12

CALORIE COUNTER

Lamb, retail cuts:
    chop, loin, lean only, broiled, 2.3 oz. with bone 122
    leg, lean and fat, roasted, boneless, 4 oz. 317
    shoulder, lean only, roasted, boneless, 4 oz. 233
Leeks, raw, 3 average 52
Lemon juice:
    fresh, 1 tbsp. 4
Lemonade, frozen, diluted, 1 cup 107
Lemons, fresh, 1 average (2⅛" diameter) 20
Lentils, whole, cooked, 1 cup 212
Lettuce:
    iceberg, 1 leaf (5" x 4½") 3
    romaine, 3 leaves (8" long) 5
Limes, fresh, 1 average (2" diameter) 19
Liverwurst, fresh, 4 oz. 348
Lobster, cooked in shell, whole, 1 lb. 112
Lobster, cooked or canned, meat only, cubed, ½ cup . 69

Macadamia nuts, 6 average nuts 104
Macaroni, boiled, drained, ½ cup 96
Macaroni and cheese, canned, ½ cup 114
Mackerel, fresh or frozen, broiled with butter, 4 oz. .. 268
Mangos, whole, 1 average (1½ per lb.) 152
Margarine, salted or unsalted, 1 tbsp. 102
Marmalade, citrus flavors, 1 tbsp. 51
Milk, chocolate, canned, with skim milk, 1 cup 190
Milk, chocolate, canned, with whole milk, 1 cup 213
Milk, cow's:
    whole, 3.5% fat, 1 cup 159
    buttermilk, cultured, 1 cup 88
    skim, 1 cup 88
    skim, partially, 1 cup 145
    canned, condensed, sweetened, 1 cup 982
    canned, evaporated, unsweetened, 1 cup 345
    dry, whole, 1 tbsp. dry form 35
    dry, nonfat, instant, 1 envelope (3.2 oz.) 327
Milk, malted, beverage, 1 cup 244
Muffin, corn, mix, made with egg, milk, 1.4 oz. muffin 130
Mushrooms, raw, sliced, chopped or diced, ½ cup ... 10
Mushrooms, canned, with liquid, ½ cup 21
Mustard greens, boiled, drained, ½ cup 16

Nectarines, fresh, 1 average (2½" diameter) 88
Noodles, chow-mein, canned, ½ cup 110
Noodles, egg, cooked, ½ cup 100

Oil, cooking or salad:
    corn, safflower, ,sesame or soy, 1 tbsp. 120
    olive or peanut, 1 tbsp. 119
Olives, pickled, canned or bottled:
    green, 10 large (¾" diameter) 45
    ripe, salt-cured, Greek style, 10 extra large 89
Onions, mature:
    raw, 1 average (2½" diameter) 40
    raw, chopped, 1 tbsp. 4
Orange juice:
    fresh, California, Valencia, 1 cup 117
    fresh, Florida, Valencia, 1 cup 112
    canned, sweetened, 1 cup 130
    canned, unsweetened, 1 cup 120
    frozen, concentrate, unsweetened, diluted, 1 cup .. 112
Oranges, fresh, 1 average 71

Pancakes, prepared from mix as directed on package:
    plain and buttermilk, 4" diameter cake 61
    buckwheat and other flours, 4" diameter cake 54
Papaya juice, canned, 1 cup 120
Papayas, fresh, whole, 1 papaya (3½" x 5⅛") 119
Peach nectar, canned, 1 cup 120
Peaches:
    fresh, 1 average 38
    canned, in juice, 2 peach halves with 2 tbsp. juice .. 45
    dried, ½ cup 210

Peanut butter, commercial, 1 tbsp. 94
Peanuts:
    roasted, in shell, 10 nuts 105
    roasted, chopped, 1 tbsp. 52
Pear nectar, canned, 1 cup 130
Pears:
    fresh, Bartlett, 1 pear (2½" diameter) 100
    canned, in heavy syrup, 1 pear half and 2 tbsp. syrup 71
    dried, ½ cup 241
Peas, green:
    boiled, drained, ½ cup 57
Peas, split, cooked, ½ cup 115
Pecans:
    shelled, 10 large nuts 62
    chopped, 1 tbsp. 52
Peppers, hot, chili:
    green, raw, seeded, 4 oz. 42
    green, chili sauce, canned, ½ cup 25
    red, chili sauce, canned, ½ cup 26
Peppers, sweet, green:
    raw, fancy grade, 1 pepper (3" diameter) 36
Peppers, sweet, red:
    raw, fancy grade, 1 pepper (3" diameter) 51
Perch, ocean, Atlantic, frozen, breaded, 4 oz. 382
Perch, white, raw, meat only, 4 oz. 134
Pickle relish:
    hamburger (Heinz), 1 tbsp. 17
    sweet, 1 tbsp. 21
Pickles, cucumber:
    dill, 1 large (4" long) 15
    sweet gherkins, 1 small (2½" long) 22
Pies, frozen:
    apple, baked, 3⅛" arc (⅛ of 8" pie) 173
    cherry, baked, 3⅛" arc (⅛ of 8" pie) 211
    coconut custard, baked, 3⅛" arc (⅛ of 8" pie) 187
Pimientos, canned, drained, 1 average 10
Pineapple:
    fresh, sliced, 1 slice (3½" diameter x ¾") 44
    canned, heavy syrup, chunks or crushed, ½ cup ... 95
    canned, water pack, tidbits, ½ cup with liquid 48
Pineapple juice, canned, unsweetened, 1 cup 138
Pistachio nuts, chopped, 1 tbsp. 53
Plums:
    damson, fresh, whole, 10 plums (1" diameter) 66
    canned, purple, 3 plums and 2¾ tbsp. liquid 110
Popcorn:
    popped, plain, 1 cup 23
    popped, with oil and salt added, 1 cup 41
Pork:
    Boston butt, lean only, roasted, 4 oz. 279
    chop, lean only, broiled, 4 oz. with bone 308
    loin, lean only, roasted, 4 oz. 288
Potato chips, 10 chips (2" diameter) 114
Potato sticks, ½ cup 95
Potatoes, white:
    baked, in skin, 1 long 145
    boiled, in skin, 1 round 104
    fried, ½ cup 228
    frozen, hash brown, cooked, ½ cup 174
    mashed, with milk and butter, ½ cup 99
Potatoes, sweet:
    baked, in skin, 1 average 161
    boiled, in skin, 1 average 172
    boiled, in skin, mashed, ½ cup 146
    candied, 1 piece (2½" long x 2") 176
Pretzels, commercial varieties:
    rods, 1 pretzel (7½" long) 55
    twisted, 3-ring, 10 pretzels 117
Prune juice, canned or bottled, 1 cup 197
Prunes, dried, medium-size, 1 average 16
Pumpkin, canned, ½ cup 41
Radishes, raw, whole, 10 medium 8
Raisins, seedless (½ cup) 210

CALORIE COUNTER

Raspberries:
  black, fresh, ½ cup 49
  red, fresh, ½ cup 35
  canned, black, water pack, 4 oz. with liquid 58
  canned, red, water pack, ½ cup with liquid 43
  frozen, red, sweetened, ½ cup 123
Rhubarb, cooked, sweetened, ½ cup 191
Rice, cooked (hot):
  brown, long grain, ½ cup 116
  white, long grain, ½ cup 112
  white, parboiled, long grain, ½ cup 93
Rolls and buns, commercial (ready to serve):
  frankfurther or hamburger, 1.4 oz. roll 119
  hard, rectangular, ⅞-oz. roll 78
  raisin, 1-oz. roll 78
  sweet, 1-oz. roll 89
  whole wheat, 1-oz. roll 73

Salad dressings, commercial:
  blue cheese, 1 tbsp. 76
  French, 1 tbsp. 66
  Italian, 1 tbsp. 83
  mayonnaise, 1 tbsp. 101
  Roquefort cheese, 1 tbsp. 76
  Russian, 1 tbsp. 74
  Thousand Island, 1 tbsp. 80
Salami:
  cooked, 1 slice (4" diameter) 68
  dry, 1 slice (3⅛" diameter) 45
Salmon, smoked, 4 oz. 200
Sauces:
  barbecue, 1 tbsp. 17
  soy, 1 tbsp. 12
  tartar, 1 tbsp. 74
  tomato, canned (Hunt's), ½ cup 35
Sauerkraut, canned, ½ cup with liquid 21
Sausages:
  polish, 2.7 oz. sausage (5⅜" long x 1" diameter) . . 231
  pork, cooked, 1 link (4" long x ⅞" diameter) 62
  pork, cooked, 1 patty (3⅞" diameter x ¼") 129
  pork and beef, chopped, 4 oz. 383
  Vienna, canned, 1 sausage (2" long) 38
Sherbet, orange, ½ cup 130
Shrimp:
  fresh, breaded, fried, 4 oz. 255
  canned, drained, 10 medium shrimp 37
Soft drinks:
  cola, 1 cup 96
  cream soda, 1 cup 105
  fruit flavored (citrus, cherry, grape, etc.), 1 cup . . . 113
  root beer, 1 cup 100
  Seven-Up, 1 cup 97
Soup, canned, condensed, diluted with equal part water:
  asparagus, cream of, 1 cup 65
  beans with pork, 1 cup 168
  beef broth, bouillon or consomme, 1 cup 31
  beef noodle, 1 cup 67
  celery, cream of, 1 cup 86
  chicken consomme, 1 cup 22
  chicken, cream of, 1 cup 94
  chicken gumbo, 1 cup 55
  chicken noodle, 1 cup 62
  chicken vegetable, 1 cup 76
  chicken with rice, 1 cup 48
  clam chowder, Manhattan type, 1 cup 81
  minestrone, 1 cup 105
  mushroom, cream of, 1 cup 134
  onion, 1 cup 65
  pea, split, 1 cup 145
  tomato, 1 cup 88
  vegetable beef, 1 cup 78
  vegetarian vegetable, 1 cup 78

Spaghetti:
  plain, boiled 8-10 minutes, drained, ½ cup 96
  canned, in tomato sauce with cheese, ½ cup 95
  canned, with meatballs in tomato sauce, ½ cup . . . 129
Spinach:
  boiled, drained, leaves, ½ cup 21
Squash, summer:
  scallop variety, boiled, drained, sliced, ½ cup 15
  yellow, boiled, drained, sliced, ½ cup 14
  zucchini, boiled, drained, sliced, ½ 11
Squash, winter:
  acorn, baked, ½ squash (4" diameter) 86
  acorn, boiled, mashed, ½ cup 42
  butternut, baked, mashed, ½ cup 70
  butternut, boiled, mashed, ½ cup 50
Strawberries:
  fresh, whole, ½ cup 28
  canned, water pack, ½ cup with liquid 27
Sugar, beet or cane:
  brown, ½ cup firm packed 411
  brown, 1 tbsp. firm packed 52
  granulated, ½ cup 385
  granulated, 1 tsp. 15
  powdered, unsifted, ½ cup 231
  powdered, stirred, 1 tbsp. 31
Sunflower seed kernels, in hull, ½ cup 129
Sunflower seed kernels, hulled, ½ cup 406
Syrups:
  chocolate, thin-type, 1 tbsp. 46
  corn, light or dark, 1 tbsp. 58
  maple, 1 tbsp. 50
  molasses, blackstrap, 1 tbsp. 43
  molasses, light, 1 tbsp. 50
  molasses, medium, 1 tbsp. 46
  sorghum, 1 tbsp. 53

Tangerines, fresh, 1 average (2⅜" diameter) 39
Tomato juice, canned or bottle, 1 cup 46
Tomato juice cocktail, canned or bottled, 1 cup 51
Tomato paste, canned, ½ cup 108
Tomato puree, canned ½ cup 49
Tomatoes, ripe:
  raw, whole, 1 average (about 2⅖" diameter) 20
  canned, ½ cup with liquid 26
Toppings: dessert:
  butterscotch, 1 tbsp. 52
  caramel, 1 tbsp. 72
  chocolate fudge, 1 tbsp. 62
  pineapple, 1 tbsp. 56
Tuna, canned:
  in oil, solid pack or chunk style, drained, ½ cup . . . 158
  in water, all styles, with liquid, 4 oz. 144
Turkey:
  dark meat, roasted, 4 oz. 230
  light meat, roasted, 4 oz. 200
  canned, boned, ½ cup 207
Turnip greens:
  fresh, boiled in small amount water, drained, ½ cup . 15
Turnips, boiled, drained, cubed, ½ cup 18

Vegetable juice cocktail, canned, 1 cup 41
Vegetables, mixed, frozen, boiled, drained, ½ cup . . . 58

Waffles, baked from mix:
  made with egg and milk, 1 round (7" diameter) 206
Walnuts, 10 large nuts 322
Watermelon, with rind, 1 wedge (4" x 8") 111
Wheat bran, commercially milled, 4 oz. 242
Wheat germ, toasted, 1 tbsp. 23

Yogurt, plain:
  partially skim milk, 8-oz. container 113
  whole milk, 8-oz. container 140

This Cookbook is a perfect gift for Holidays, Weddings, Anniversaries & Birthdays.

To order extra copies as gifts for your friends, please use Order Forms on reverse side of this page.

* * * * * * * * * *

Cookbook Publishers, Inc. has published millions of personalized cookbooks for every kind of organization from every state in the union. We are pleased to have the privilege of publishing this fine cookbook.

ORDER FORM

Use the order forms below for obtaining
additional copies of this cookbook.

Fill in Order Forms Below - Cut Out and Mail

You may order as many copies of our Cookbook as you wish for the regular price, plus
$2.55 postage and packing per book ordered. Mail to:

**Ruthie Wornall
9800 West 104th St.
Overland Park, KS   66212**

Please mail _____ copies of your Cookbook @ $14.95 each, plus $2.55 postage
and packing per book ordered.

Mail books to:

Name _____

Address _____

City, State, Zip _____

You may order as many copies of our Cookbook as you wish for the regular price, plus
$2.55 postage and packing per book ordered. Mail to:

**Ruthie Wornall
9800 West 104th St.
Overland Park, KS   66212**

Please mail _____ copies of your Cookbook @ $14.95 each, plus $2.55 postage
and packing per book ordered.

Mail books to:

Name _____

Address _____

City, State, Zip _____